HECTIC

BUT

Holy

A 52 WEEK DEVOTIONAL
JOURNAL FOR VERY BUSY WOMEN

TAYLOR BRIONE BALLARD

Published by Taylor B. Ballard, www.taylorbrione.com

1919 Taylor Street Ste F #1033 Houston, TX 77077

Cover Design: Getcovers

Interior Design: Winn Publications

Editor: Nicole Boccelli-Saltsman

Dedication

To Mommy, Daddy, and my sisters, Hollye, Morgan, Loren, Hope, and Hannah,

Your unwavering love, support, and encouragement have been a light on my path, even in my darkest, most uncertain, and busiest times. You all have been the guiding stars that help this very busy girl shine her brightest.

Thank you for being my constant source of strength and inspiration. This book is dedicated to you with all my love and gratitude.

Love y'all!

Taylor Brione Ballard

Introduction

I discovered I was busy at a young age. I remember being in fourth grade, writing down all of the things I had to do for school and my after school clubs. I was only 10.

School, work, sports, activities, church, social life, family time—it never seemed to slow down, and as I got older, it actually became worse!

Throughout my crazy busy life, I learned something very important---in order to handle all of the demands of life, I needed strength beyond my own, strength that could only come from God. I also realized that when I neglected my devotion, my relationship with God struggled,causing every aspect of my life to follow.

I wrote "Hectic But Holy" not as an expert from a girl who has her life altogether but rather a guide for others who are just figuring it out day by day. This book should serve as a reminder that even on your most busy days, there is still room for devotion, prayer, and worship. Even throughout the hectic, there is always space for holy.

If you have ever felt the weight of a truly packed calendar, longed for deep and intimate moments with God, this book was written for you. It's a reflection of my own journey and a guide for yours.

Week 1: Balance and Priorities

"But seek first His kingdom and His righteousness, and
all these things will be given to you as well."

Matthew 6:33 (NIV)

Many of us juggle a lot of responsibilities, from work to
family and personal goals. We strive to bring out the best
of us while tackling each responsibility. However, as we
do this, we may easily lose sight of our true purpose: the
pursuit of God's kingdom. As women of God, we need to
find a balance between our responsibility and our devotion
to God. How do we find time to connect with God amid
our busy schedules? Between our responsibilities and
a quiet time with God, what is more important? Jesus
doesn't ask us to neglect our responsibilities. Rather, He
instructs us to prioritize our relationship with God more
than anything else. This instruction comes with a special
promise: 'all other things will be given to us as well.'
God will grant us the grace and strength to handle our

responsibilities with peace. So, if we really want to attract the grace that will help us in navigating our busy schedules, let us strive to begin each day with God. Read a scripture, pray, and seek God's face through worship. Let God be at the center of your work, interactions, and your pursuits.

Prayer

Dear Lord, in the midst of my busy and hectic lifestyle, help me seek first your kingdom and righteousness. I desire to start each day with you, O Lord: to start the day with your love, grace, and guidance. Guide my steps and choices so that everything I do aligns with your will. Help me to prioritize you, even when I am faced with countless responsibilities. I pray for the wisdom to find balance and the grace to glorify you in all I undertake. In Jesus' name, I pray. Amen.

Related Scriptures for the Week

Proverbs 3:6 (NIV):

"In all your ways submit to him, and he will make your paths straight."

Psalm 37:4 (NIV):

"Take delight in the Lord, and he will give you the desires of your heart."

Psalm 63:1 (NIV):

"You, God, are my God, earnestly I seek you; I thirst for you, my whole being longs for you, in a dry and parched land where there is no water."

Colossians 3:1-2 (NIV):

"Since, then, you have been raised with Christ, set your hearts on things above, where Christ is, seated at the right hand of God. Set your minds on things above, not on earthly things."

1 Chronicles 28:9 (NIV):

"And you, my son Solomon, acknowledge the God of your father, and serve him with wholehearted devotion and with a willing mind, for the Lord searches every heart and understands every desire and every thought. If you seek him, he will be found by you; but if you forsake him, he will reject you forever."

Psalm 105:4 (NIV):

"Look to the Lord and his strength; seek his face always."

Proverbs 8:17 (NIV):

"I love those who love me, and those who seek me find me."

Isaiah 55:6 (NIV):

"Seek the Lord while he may be found; call on him while he is near."

Prayer Tracker

WEEK OF: / /

PRAYER REQUEST	S	M	T	W	T	F	S
_____	●	●	●	●	●	●	●
_____	●	●	●	●	●	●	●
_____	●	●	●	●	●	●	●
_____	●	●	●	●	●	●	●
_____	●	●	●	●	●	●	●
_____	●	●	●	●	●	●	●
_____	●	●	●	●	●	●	●
_____	●	●	●	●	●	●	●
_____	●	●	●	●	●	●	●
_____	●	●	●	●	●	●	●
_____	●	●	●	●	●	●	●
_____	●	●	●	●	●	●	●
_____	●	●	●	●	●	●	●

NOTES

_____

_____

_____

_____

_____

_____

_____

Week 2: Balance and Priorities

"You shall have no other gods before me.

Exodus 20:3 (NIV)

As we try to fulfill our daily responsibilities, we may unknowingly elevate various pursuits, possessions, or even people to the place of God. When we do this, we make these pursuits our 'gods' since anything that takes the place of God is a god. Yet, God's commandment is very clear: "You shall have no other gods before me." It reminds us that we must evaluate where we place our trust and devotion. As we struggle to find a perfect balance between our devotion to God and our commitment to our responsibilities, we must remember that God desires to be at the forefront. We must prioritize Him above all else and let Him guide our paths. As women of God, let us examine our hearts today. Are there things, people, or pursuits that have taken precedence over God? Let us take a moment to realign our priorities and put God

back in His rightful place. This step of faith will not end up in vain and neither will it make us have less time to manage our responsibilities. Instead, as we do this, we will find that life issues will become more manageable.

Prayer

Heavenly Father, I ask for your forgiveness for all the times that I prioritized my daily responsibilities and pursuits over you. Forgive me for the times I let my life's issues become my gods. Lord, help me center my life on you. I acknowledge you as my only True God, and I will strive to worship you alone from today and going forward. May my priorities reflect your rightful place in my heart. In Jesus' name, I pray. Amen.

Related Scriptures for the Week

Deuteronomy 6:4-5 (NIV):

"Hear, O Israel: The Lord our God, the Lord is one. Love the Lord your God with all your heart and with all your soul and with all your strength."

Joshua 24:14 (NIV):

"Now fear the Lord and serve him with all faithfulness. Throw away the gods your ancestors worshiped beyond the Euphrates River and in Egypt, and serve the Lord."

1 Corinthians 8:4 (NIV):

"So then, about eating food sacrificed to idols: We know that 'An idol is nothing at all in the world' and that 'There is no God but one.'"

1 John 5:21 (NIV):

"Dear children, keep yourselves from idols."

Psalm 81:9 (NIV):

"You shall have no foreign god among you; you shall not worship any god other than me."

1 Samuel 7:3 (NIV):

"Then Samuel said to all the people of Israel, 'If you are returning to the Lord with all your hearts, then rid yourselves of the foreign gods and the Ashtoreths and commit yourselves to the Lord and serve him only, and he will deliver you out of the hand of the Philistines.'"

Isaiah 42:8 (NIV):

"I am the Lord; that is my name! I will not yield my glory to another or my praise to idols."

Prayer Tracker

WEEK OF: / /

PRAYER REQUEST	S	M	T	W	T	F	S
_____	●	●	●	●	●	●	●
_____	●	●	●	●	●	●	●
_____	●	●	●	●	●	●	●
_____	●	●	●	●	●	●	●
_____	●	●	●	●	●	●	●
_____	●	●	●	●	●	●	●
_____	●	●	●	●	●	●	●
_____	●	●	●	●	●	●	●
_____	●	●	●	●	●	●	●
_____	●	●	●	●	●	●	●
_____	●	●	●	●	●	●	●
_____	●	●	●	●	●	●	●
_____	●	●	●	●	●	●	●

NOTES

_____

_____

_____

_____

_____

_____

_____

Week 3: Balance and Priorities

"Do not lay up for yourselves treasures on earth, where moth and rust destroy and where thieves break in and steal."

Matthew 6:19 (NIV)

As women, we are expected to do our best if we want to prosper in life. Success and prosperity come to those who are committed and persistent in what they do. But do we even realize that the pursuit of worldly treasures can easily consume our thoughts and actions and make us forget about what matters most? When we put all our efforts in accumulating possessions, security, and fulfillment to an extent that we have no time for God, we are only storing up temporary treasures. Material possessions are good, but they are temporary and susceptible to loss and decay. Worldly treasures cannot grant us eternal satisfaction. True balance in the life of a Godly woman is found in our devotion to God. We store heavenly and eternal treasures for ourselves when we serve God and prioritize spending quiet time in His presence. Where do you invest your time, energy, and resources? If you want to find balance, fulfillment, and true satisfaction, then you must align your priorities with God's will. As you strive for success, growth, and prosperity, do not forget to also strive for the things that further the kingdom of God.

Prayer

Loving Father, thank you for loving me and for making me an heir to your heavenly kingdom. Thank you for loving me so much that you gave your only Son to die for my redemption and salvation. To acknowledge the love you have shown towards me, I want to wholeheartedly devote my heart to you. Help me not to be consumed by the pursuit of earthly treasures but to seek after your heart. I pray that you may guide me to invest in things that bring eternal satisfaction and fulfillment. In Jesus' name, I pray. Amen.

Related Scriptures for the Week

Luke 12:33-34 (NIV):

"Sell your possessions and give to the poor. Provide purses for yourselves that will not wear out, a treasure in heaven that will never fail, where no thief comes near and no moth destroys. For where your treasure is, there your heart will be also."

1 Timothy 6:17-19 (NIV):

"Command those who are rich in this present world not to be arrogant nor to put their hope in wealth, which is so uncertain, but to put their hope in God, who richly provides us with everything for our enjoyment. Command them to do good, to be rich in good deeds, and to be generous and willing to share. In this way they will lay up treasure for themselves as a firm foundation for the coming age, so that they may take hold of the life that is truly life."

Mark 8:36-37 (NIV):

"What good is it for someone to gain the whole world, yet forfeit their soul? Or what can anyone give in exchange for their soul?"

Proverbs 23:4-5 (NIV):

"Do not wear yourself out to get rich; do not trust your own cleverness. Cast but a glance at riches, and they are gone, for they will surely sprout wings and fly off to the sky like an eagle."

Ecclesiastes 5:10 (NIV):

"Whoever loves money never has enough; whoever loves wealth is never satisfied with their income. This too is meaningless."

Hebrews 13:5 (NIV):

"Keep your lives free from the love of money and be content with what you have because God has said, 'Never will I leave you; never will I forsake you.'"

1 John 2:15-17 (NIV):

"Do not love the world or anything in the world. If anyone loves the world, love for the Father is not in them. For everything in the world—the lust of the flesh, the lust of the eyes, and the pride of life—comes not from the Father but from the world. The world and its desires pass away, but whoever does the will of God lives forever."

Prayer Tracker

WEEK OF: / /

PRAYER REQUEST

	S	M	T	W	T	F	S
_____	●	●	●	●	●	●	●
_____	●	●	●	●	●	●	●
_____	●	●	●	●	●	●	●
_____	●	●	●	●	●	●	●
_____	●	●	●	●	●	●	●
_____	●	●	●	●	●	●	●
_____	●	●	●	●	●	●	●
_____	●	●	●	●	●	●	●
_____	●	●	●	●	●	●	●
_____	●	●	●	●	●	●	●
_____	●	●	●	●	●	●	●
_____	●	●	●	●	●	●	●
_____	●	●	●	●	●	●	●

NOTES

_____

_____

_____

_____

_____

_____

_____

Week 4: Balance and Priorities

"Flee the evil desires of youth and pursue righteousness, faith, love, and peace, along with those who call on the Lord out of a pure heart."

2 Timothy 2:22 (NIV)

It is normal for every woman to have their different passions, leisure activities, goals, and ambitions. All these can make our lives hectic, but we can pursue and seek holiness amid them all. Finding balance in situations like these requires us to make intentional choices. We must resist the allure of worldly pleasures and focus on pursuits that build our relationship with God. The pursuit of righteousness and a deeper connection with God should be our main goal. This may involve having time to fellowship with other believers, listening to sermons, worshipping, and praying. When you reflect upon your lifestyle and how you navigate through your daily hustle and bustles, do you see anything that you feel you need to flee from? Do you notice anything that is denying you the opportunity to seek after heavenly things? God wants us to embrace the call to pursue righteousness, faith, love, and peace. Respond to the call and experience a purpose-filled life.

Prayer

Gracious Lord, I pray for the strength and wisdom to flee from my passions and fleshly desires and to pursue the virtues that align with your kingdom. I invite you to reign over every aspect of my life and take charge of every minute of my life. May my life bring glory and honor back to you through every activity that I do. In Jesus' name, Amen.

Related Scriptures for the Week

1 Corinthians 6:18 (NIV):

"Flee from sexual immorality. All other sins a person commits are outside the body, but whoever sins sexually, sins against their own body."

Proverbs 4:23 (NIV):

"Above all else, guard your heart, for everything you do flows from it."

1 Timothy 6:11 (NIV):

"But you, man of God, flee from all this, and pursue righteousness, godliness, faith, love, endurance, and gentleness."

1 Corinthians 10:14 (NIV):

"Therefore, my dear friends, flee from idolatry."

Ephesians 4:22-24 (NIV):

"You were taught, with regard to your former way of life, to put off your old self, which is being corrupted by its deceitful desires; to be made new in the attitude of your minds; and to put on the new self, created to be like God in true righteousness and holiness."

1 Peter 3:11 (NIV):

"They must turn from evil and do good; they must seek peace and pursue it."

James 4:7-8 (NIV):

"Submit yourselves, then, to God. Resist the devil, and he will flee from you. Come near to God, and he will come near to you. Wash your hands, you sinners, and purify your hearts, you double-minded."

1 Timothy 4:12 (NIV):

"Don't let anyone look down on you because you are young, but set an example for the believers in speech, in conduct, in love, in faith and in purity."

Prayer Tracker

WEEK OF: / /

PRAYER REQUEST	S	M	T	W	T	F	S
_____	○	○	○	○	○	○	○
_____	○	○	○	○	○	○	○
_____	○	○	○	○	○	○	○
_____	○	○	○	○	○	○	○
_____	○	○	○	○	○	○	○
_____	○	○	○	○	○	○	○
_____	○	○	○	○	○	○	○
_____	○	○	○	○	○	○	○
_____	○	○	○	○	○	○	○
_____	○	○	○	○	○	○	○
_____	○	○	○	○	○	○	○
_____	○	○	○	○	○	○	○
_____	○	○	○	○	○	○	○

NOTES

_____

_____

_____

_____

_____

_____

_____

Week 5: Balance and Priorities

"Whatever you do, work at it with all your heart, as working for the Lord, not for human masters."

Colossians 3:23 (NIV)

Balancing a hectic life often involves managing work and responsibilities wisely. Amid our tasks, it is important for us to work with an attitude that reflects the image of the Lord. In Colossians 3:23, we are asked to be women who will reflect God's glory and honor in daily responsibilities. Our daily tasks, whether in our professions, at our homes, or in ministry, are an opportunity to serve the Lord. Let's not be women who will always use our busy schedules as excuses not to work on our relationship with God. We can always grow closer to Him by working with hearts that are dedicated to Him. When we approach our tasks with dedication and hearts that seek to honor God, we prove our devotion and love for Him. Therefore, as we navigate the demands of life, let us offer our responsibilities as a form of worship to the Lord. May we always seek His guidance in our tasks and commit our efforts to Him.

Prayer

Almighty God, thank you for the ability to work and the strength that you have given me to handle different tasks. I thank you for my job, my business, and all other responsibilities that you have bestowed upon me. Lord, I pray that you help me work with all my heart as if working for you and not for human recognition. Anytime you see me trying to seek the attention of mankind or to fulfill my own desires through my responsibilities, remind me of your Word in Colossians 3:23. May all my daily tasks be an offering of worship to you and a channel through which I will edify and glorify your name. In Jesus' name, I pray. Amen.

Related Scriptures for the Week

Ephesians 6:7-8 (NIV):

"Serve wholeheartedly, as if you were serving the Lord, not people, because you know that the Lord will reward each one for whatever good they do, whether they are slave or free."

1 Corinthians 10:31 (NIV):

"So whether you eat or drink or whatever you do, do it all for the glory of God."

Proverbs 16:3 (NIV):

"Commit to the Lord whatever you do, and he will establish your plans."

Proverbs 22:29 (NIV):

"Do you see someone skilled in their work? They will serve before kings; they will not serve before officials of low rank."

Colossians 3:17 (NIV):

"And whatever you do, whether in word or deed, do it all in the name of the Lord Jesus, giving thanks to God the Father through him."

Proverbs 14:23 (NIV):

"All hard work brings a profit, but mere talk leads only to poverty."

2 Thessalonians 3:10 (NIV):

"For even when we were with you, we gave you this rule: 'The one who is unwilling to work shall not eat.'"

Ecclesiastes 9:10 (NIV):

"Whatever your hand finds to do, do it with all your might, for in the realm of the dead, where you are going, there is neither working nor planning nor knowledge nor wisdom."

Prayer Tracker

WEEK OF: / /

PRAYER REQUEST	S	M	T	W	T	F	S
_____	●	●	●	●	●	●	●
_____	●	●	●	●	●	●	●
_____	●	●	●	●	●	●	●
_____	●	●	●	●	●	●	●
_____	●	●	●	●	●	●	●
_____	●	●	●	●	●	●	●
_____	●	●	●	●	●	●	●
_____	●	●	●	●	●	●	●
_____	●	●	●	●	●	●	●
_____	●	●	●	●	●	●	●
_____	●	●	●	●	●	●	●
_____	●	●	●	●	●	●	●
_____	●	●	●	●	●	●	●

NOTES

_____

_____

_____

_____

_____

_____

Week 6: Balance and Priorities

"There is a time for everything and a season for every activity under the heavens."

Ecclesiastes 3:1 (NIV)

As busy women, we carry a lot on our shoulders and our schedules may always seem tight. The many responsibilities that we have can make us feel like we are constantly racing against time. However, God, in Ecclesiastes 3:1 reminds us that there is a time for everything. He created time and seasons so that we could find a balance for all activities under the heavens. The time and seasons are meant to help us balance and choose which responsibilities to prioritize in our lives at the moment in time. Since we are women of God, we must take comfort in knowing that God has appointed specific times and seasons for every aspect of our lives. There is a time to work and a time to rest. We must also know what time to dedicate ourselves to our responsibilities and what time to dedicate ourselves to God. Each of these contributes to our growth and purpose. May we always seek the guidance of the Holy Spirit in knowing what time is best for which activity.

Prayer

Dear Lord, thank you for all the seasons and time that you have appointed to every activity under the sun. My heart desires to align all my tasks and responsibilities to the time and seasons that you have created. I pray for the wisdom to discern every season of my life and the grace to make good use of every minute. Help me, dear Lord, to find balance in your perfect timing and plan. In Jesus' name, I pray. Amen.

Related Scriptures for the Week

Proverbs 15:23 (NIV):

"A person finds joy in giving an apt reply—and how good is a timely word!"

Psalm 31:15 (NIV):

"My times are in your hands; deliver me from the hands of my enemies, from those who pursue me."

Galatians 6:9 (NIV):

"Let us not become weary in doing good, for at the proper time we will reap a harvest if we do not give up."

Psalm 104:19 (NIV):

"He made the moon to mark the seasons, and the sun knows when to go down."

1 Peter 5:6 (NIV):

"Humble yourselves, therefore, under God's mighty hand, that he may lift you up in due time."

Lamentations 3:22-23 (NIV):

"Because of the Lord's great love we are not consumed, for his compassions never fail. They are new every morning; great is your faithfulness."

Genesis 8:22 (NIV):

"As long as the earth endures, seedtime and harvest, cold and heat, summer and winter, day and night will never cease."

Prayer Tracker

WEEK OF: / /

PRAYER REQUEST	S	M	T	W	T	F	S
_____	○	○	○	○	○	○	○
_____	○	○	○	○	○	○	○
_____	○	○	○	○	○	○	○
_____	○	○	○	○	○	○	○
_____	○	○	○	○	○	○	○
_____	○	○	○	○	○	○	○
_____	○	○	○	○	○	○	○
_____	○	○	○	○	○	○	○
_____	○	○	○	○	○	○	○
_____	○	○	○	○	○	○	○
_____	○	○	○	○	○	○	○
_____	○	○	○	○	○	○	○
_____	○	○	○	○	○	○	○

NOTES

_____

_____

_____

_____

_____

_____

_____

Week 7: Rest in Chaos

"Who of you by worrying can add a single hour to your life? Since you cannot do this very little thing, why do you worry about the rest?"

Luke 12:25-26 (NIV)

Amid the chaos and busyness that surrounds our lives, anxiety can easily creep in. We often find ourselves worrying about the huge burdens on our shoulders. And most times, we feel overwhelmed by the thought of what we have to accomplish. These states of worry and anxiety can make us feel weary and broken and oftentimes, like we have failed. We may experience emotional roller coasters or lose sleep over things that don't seem to work out the way we want. But this is not what God desires for His precious daughters. God wants us to stay calm and free our minds from any thoughts that can drive us into a state of anxiety. Worrying or being anxious does not add a single moment to our lives. It drains our energy and steals our peace. This is why God invites us to fully trust in Him. By surrendering our anxieties to Him, we experience the rest we need amid the chaos of life. So, let go of the burdens that weigh on your heart. Surrender your burdens to God through prayer and seek His guidance.

Prayer

Heavenly Father, I thank you for being in control over every aspect of my life. I repent of all the times that I have been trying to take full control over my life. I admit that this has only led to feelings of anxiety, fear, and worry. But I now release them all to you for I know that your care surpasses all understanding. I ask that you grant me the peace that comes from trusting in your sovereignty. May I find rest in the knowledge that you are in control and will make everything fall into its rightful place at your appointed time. In Jesus' name, I pray. Amen.

Related Scriptures for the Week

Philippians 4:6-7 (NIV):

"Do not be anxious about anything, but in every situation, by prayer and petition, with thanksgiving, present your requests to God. And the peace of God, which transcends all understanding, will guard your hearts and your minds in Christ Jesus."

Matthew 6:25-27 (NIV):

"Therefore I tell you, do not worry about your life, what you will eat or drink; or about your body, what you will wear. Is not life more than food, and the body more than clothes? Look at the birds of the air; they do not sow or reap or store away in barns, and yet your heavenly Father feeds them. Are you not much more valuable than they? Can any one of you by worrying add a single hour to your life?"

Psalm 55:22 (NIV):

"Cast your cares on the Lord and he will sustain you; he will never let the righteous be shaken."

1 Peter 5:7 (NIV):

"Cast all your anxiety on him because he cares for you."

Isaiah 41:10 (NIV):

"So do not fear, for I am with you; do not be dismayed, for I am your God. I will strengthen you and help you; I will uphold you with my righteous right hand."

Matthew 11:28-30 (NIV):

"Come to me, all you who are weary and burdened, and I will give you rest. Take my yoke upon you and learn from me, for I am gentle and humble in heart, and you will find rest for your souls. For my yoke is easy and my burden is light."

2 Timothy 1:7 (NIV):

"For the Spirit God gave us does not make us timid, but gives us power, love and self-discipline."

Psalm 37:7 (NIV):

"Be still before the Lord and wait patiently for him; do not fret when people succeed in their ways, when they carry out their wicked schemes."

Prayer Tracker

WEEK OF: / /

PRAYER REQUEST	S	M	T	W	T	F	S
_____	●	●	●	●	●	●	●
_____	●	●	●	●	●	●	●
_____	●	●	●	●	●	●	●
_____	●	●	●	●	●	●	●
_____	●	●	●	●	●	●	●
_____	●	●	●	●	●	●	●
_____	●	●	●	●	●	●	●
_____	●	●	●	●	●	●	●
_____	●	●	●	●	●	●	●
_____	●	●	●	●	●	●	●
_____	●	●	●	●	●	●	●
_____	●	●	●	●	●	●	●
_____	●	●	●	●	●	●	●

NOTES

_____

_____

_____

_____

_____

_____

_____

Week 8: Rest in Chaos

"When anxiety was great within me, your consolation brought me joy."

Psalm 94:19 (NIV)

Life can bring an abundance of cares and worries. The weight of responsibilities, challenges, and uncertainties can often overwhelm us. But we should take heart because God's consolations are there to cheer our souls. His promises, encouraging words, and words of hope are meant to inspire us and bring us to a state of peace. Amid the chaos of life and when our hearts are burdened, we can always turn to the inspiration of the Word of God. His consolations, found in His Word and through prayer, bring solace and refreshment to our weary souls. They are the best antidote prescriptions to our anxieties and stress. We are not alone in the chaos that surrounds our lives. We have God, a Father who cares so much and who always wants the best for us. Draw closer to Him and allow His comforting presence to bring cheer to your soul every day.

Prayer

Compassionate God, I thank you for loving me beyond measure and for your endless concern. I'm grateful for your promise and assurance that you will console my heart when the cares of life overwhelm me. Direct me to the consolation of your Word every time you see me feeling anxious and restless. When life's pressures overwhelm me, remind me to seek comfort in you. I ask that you fill my heart with your presence and bring cheer to my soul in the midst of life's chaos. In Jesus' name, I pray. Amen.

Related Scriptures for the Week

Psalm 34:17-18 (NIV):

"The righteous cry out, and the Lord hears them; he delivers them from all their troubles. The Lord is close to the brokenhearted and saves those who are crushed in spirit."

Psalm 55:22 (NIV):

"Cast your cares on the Lord and he will sustain you; he will never let the righteous be shaken."

2 Corinthians 1:3-4 (NIV):

"Praise be to the God and Father of our Lord Jesus Christ, the Father of compassion and the God of all comfort, who comforts us in all our troubles, so that we can comfort those in any trouble with the comfort we ourselves receive from God."

Isaiah 41:10 (NIV):

"So do not fear, for I am with you; do not be dismayed, for I am your God. I will strengthen you and help you; I will uphold you with my righteous right hand."

John 14:27 (NIV):

"Peace I leave with you; my peace I give you. I do not give to you as the world gives. Do not let your hearts be troubled and do not be afraid."

1 Peter 5:7 (NIV):

"Cast all your anxiety on him because he cares for you."

Prayer Tracker

WEEK OF: / /

PRAYER REQUEST

	S	M	T	W	T	F	S
_____	●	●	●	●	●	●	●
_____	●	●	●	●	●	●	●
_____	●	●	●	●	●	●	●
_____	●	●	●	●	●	●	●
_____	●	●	●	●	●	●	●
_____	●	●	●	●	●	●	●
_____	●	●	●	●	●	●	●
_____	●	●	●	●	●	●	●
_____	●	●	●	●	●	●	●
_____	●	●	●	●	●	●	●
_____	●	●	●	●	●	●	●
_____	●	●	●	●	●	●	●
_____	●	●	●	●	●	●	●

NOTES

_____

_____

_____

_____

_____

_____

_____

Week 9: Rest in Chaos

"Even though I walk through the darkest valley, I will fear no evil, for you are with me; your rod and your staff, they comfort me."

Psalm 23:4 (NIV)

Life's journey may take us through dark valleys: moments of hardship, loss, uncertainty, and fear. From the weariness that comes from juggling different responsibilities to the fear of the unknown and the failures we experience in our lives, life can feel like a shadow of death. We may experience situations that may seem like an unending dark night. However, we should not allow the chaos in the world to cut our lives, peace, and happiness short. We have a loving and caring Father who is always with us. He is a great shepherd who keeps watch over us day and night. Even in the darkest valley, God is with us to guide, protect, and provide for us. The presence of God brings light to the darkest moments of our lives. He provides comfort, hope, and assurance amid the chaos of life. We need not fear the evil that surrounds us for He has never left our side, and He never will.

Prayer

Dear Lord, I thank you for your endless presence in my life. Thank you for being my shepherd, a source of guidance, direction, protection, and provision. Even when I am faced with struggles, chaos, and uncertainty, your presence gives me hope and comfort. With you by my side, I am assured of divine protection and provision. From today henceforth, I will not be afraid of anything that comes my way because I know that you are with me. May your Spirit guide me to always seek your comfort and protection amid the chaos that surrounds me. In Jesus' name, I pray. Amen.

Related Scriptures for the Week

Deuteronomy 31:6 (NIV):

"Be strong and courageous. Do not be afraid or terrified because of them, for the Lord your God goes with you; he will never leave you nor forsake you."

Isaiah 43:2 (NIV):

"When you pass through the waters, I will be with you; and when you pass through the rivers, they will not sweep over you. When you walk through the fire, you will not be burned; the flames will not set you ablaze."

Psalm 27:1 (NIV):

"The Lord is my light and my salvation—whom shall I fear? The Lord is the stronghold of my life—of whom shall I be afraid?"

2 Timothy 1:7 (NIV):

"For the Spirit God gave us does not make us timid, but gives us power, love, and self-discipline."

Psalm 46:1 (NIV):

"God is our refuge and strength, an ever-present help in trouble."

Matthew 28:20 (NIV):

"And surely I am with you always, to the very end of the age."

Romans 8:38-39 (NIV):

"For I am convinced that neither death nor life, neither angels nor demons, neither the present nor the future, nor any powers, neither height nor depth, nor anything else in all creation, will be able to separate us from the love of God that is in Christ Jesus our Lord."

Prayer Tracker

WEEK OF: / /

PRAYER REQUEST	S	M	T	W	T	F	S
_____	●	●	●	●	●	●	●
_____	●	●	●	●	●	●	●
_____	●	●	●	●	●	●	●
_____	●	●	●	●	●	●	●
_____	●	●	●	●	●	●	●
_____	●	●	●	●	●	●	●
_____	●	●	●	●	●	●	●
_____	●	●	●	●	●	●	●
_____	●	●	●	●	●	●	●
_____	●	●	●	●	●	●	●
_____	●	●	●	●	●	●	●
_____	●	●	●	●	●	●	●
_____	●	●	●	●	●	●	●

NOTES

_____

_____

_____

_____

_____

_____

_____

Week 10: Rest in Chaos

"So do not be afraid of them, for there is nothing concealed that will not be disclosed, or hidden that will not be made known."

Matthew 10:26 (NIV)

Life often presents situations where things remain concealed and hidden from us. This may happen at our homes, in our neighborhoods, at our places of work, and even at places where we run our business. Such things are always done in secret because they are meant to harm and bring us down. They are done by our enemies or friends and family who want no good for us. This is why it is always important to pray for the protection of the Lord regardless of how busy we are. You never know who wants to see you destroyed; it could be an enemy masquerading as a good friend. God has a way of bringing forth truth and light. We must set aside time to communicate with God and listen to His still and gentle voice. God does not ask us to fight back but to find rest and calm in Him. In due time, He will reveal all things that were done in secret for our ruin. In times of chaos and confusion, we can find solace in the truth that God unveils what is concealed. He brings clarity to confusion and reveals what is hidden in darkness. Therefore, we need not fear the unknown. Instead, let us devote ourselves to God and trust that He will bring everything to light when the time comes.

Prayer

Heavenly Father, your Word assures us that when we call unto you, you will hear us and reveal to us the things we knew nothing about. I acknowledge that sometimes I am faced with situations I know nothing about. Sometimes I fall short of ways when trying to figure out how I can go about certain issues affecting my life. But I trust you, Lord, and I surrender my hidden fears and concerns to you. Thank you for the promise that nothing remains concealed forever. I pray that you may grant me peace and rest in knowing that you will bring every hidden thing concerning my life to light. In Jesus' name, I pray. Amen.

Related Scriptures for the Week

Luke 12:2-3 (NIV):

"There is nothing concealed that will not be disclosed, or hidden that will not be made known. What you have said in the dark will be heard in the daylight, and what you have whispered in the ear in the inner rooms will be proclaimed from the roofs."

1 Corinthians 4:5 (NIV):

"Therefore judge nothing before the appointed time; wait until the Lord comes. He will bring to light what is hidden in darkness and will expose the motives of the heart. At that time, each will receive their praise from God."

Mark 4:22 (NIV):

"For whatever is hidden is meant to be disclosed, and whatever is concealed is meant to be brought out into the open."

Luke 8:17 (NIV):

"For there is nothing hidden that will not be disclosed, and nothing concealed that will not be known or brought out into the open."

1 Samuel 16:7 (NIV):

"But the Lord said to Samuel, 'Do not consider his appearance or his height, for I have rejected him. The Lord does not look at the things people look at. People look at the outward appearance, but the Lord looks at the heart.'"

Romans 8:31 (NIV):

"What, then, shall we say in response to these things? If God is for us, who can be against us?"

Psalm 56:4 (NIV):

"In God, whose word I praise—in God I trust and am not afraid. What can mere mortals do to me?"

Prayer Tracker

WEEK OF: / /

PRAYER REQUEST	S	M	T	W	T	F	S
_____	○	○	○	○	○	○	○
_____	○	○	○	○	○	○	○
_____	○	○	○	○	○	○	○
_____	○	○	○	○	○	○	○
_____	○	○	○	○	○	○	○
_____	○	○	○	○	○	○	○
_____	○	○	○	○	○	○	○
_____	○	○	○	○	○	○	○
_____	○	○	○	○	○	○	○
_____	○	○	○	○	○	○	○
_____	○	○	○	○	○	○	○
_____	○	○	○	○	○	○	○
_____	○	○	○	○	○	○	○

NOTES

_____

_____

_____

_____

_____

_____

_____

Week 11: Self-Care

"Don't you know that you yourselves are God's temple and that God's Spirit dwells in your midst?"

1 Corinthians 3:16 (NIV)

In our hectic lives, we often forget to take good care of ourselves. We focus all our attention on achieving our dreams and goals and forget about self-care. Most times, we keep postponing and canceling the schedules we make for self-care. We forget that we matter and we need time for ourselves. Many women are too busy to recognize that their bodies are God's temple. The Lord's Spirit dwells within us, and our bodies are sacred dwelling places for the Lord. Just as we care for our homes, we must prioritize self-care. We must nourish our bodies, minds, and souls with rest, healthy choices, and moments of stillness. As we do this, we not only take care of our bodies, but we express our honor to the Spirit of God that dwells within our bodies. So, ladies, take a step towards self-care. Treat yourself with the same love and care you would give to a sacred temple because that is what you are.

Prayer

Heavenly Father, amid the pressures of life, help me remember that I am your sacred dwelling place. I pray for your grace, guidance, and direction in prioritizing self-care and honoring your presence within me. Grant me wisdom in nurturing my body, mind, and soul. Help me to find a balance between my daily responsibilities and self-care. I thank you for every part of my body, and I purpose to take good care of my body from today henceforth. In Jesus' name, I pray. Amen.

Related Scriptures for the Week

2 Corinthians 6:16 (NIV):

"What agreement is there between the temple of God and idols? For we are the temple of the living God. As God has said: 'I will live with them and walk among them, and I will be their God, and they will be my people.'"

Ephesians 2:21-22 (NIV):

"In him the whole building is joined together and rises to become a holy temple in the Lord. And in him you too are being built together to become a dwelling in which God lives by his Spirit."

Romans 8:9 (NIV):

"You, however, are not in the realm of the flesh but are in the realm of the Spirit, if indeed the Spirit of God lives in you. And if anyone does not have the Spirit of Christ, they do not belong to Christ.

1 Peter 2:5 (NIV):

"You also, like living stones, are being built into a spiritual house to be a holy priesthood, offering spiritual sacrifices acceptable to God through Jesus Christ."

John 14:16-17 (NIV):

"And I will ask the Father, and he will give you another advocate to help you and be with you forever—the Spirit of truth. The world cannot accept him because it neither sees him nor knows him. But you know him, for he lives with you and will be in you."

1 John 4:13 (NIV):

"This is how we know that we live in him and he in us: He has given us of his Spirit."

Prayer Tracker

WEEK OF: / /

PRAYER REQUEST

	S	M	T	W	T	F	S
_____	○	○	○	○	○	○	○
_____	○	○	○	○	○	○	○
_____	○	○	○	○	○	○	○
_____	○	○	○	○	○	○	○
_____	○	○	○	○	○	○	○
_____	○	○	○	○	○	○	○
_____	○	○	○	○	○	○	○
_____	○	○	○	○	○	○	○
_____	○	○	○	○	○	○	○
_____	○	○	○	○	○	○	○
_____	○	○	○	○	○	○	○
_____	○	○	○	○	○	○	○
_____	○	○	○	○	○	○	○

NOTES

_____

_____

_____

_____

_____

_____

_____

Week 12: Self-Care

"Do you not know that your bodies are temples of the Holy Spirit, who is in you, whom you have received from God? You are not your own; you were bought at a price. Therefore, honor God with your bodies."

1 Corinthians 6:19-20 (NIV)

As women, our lives are characterized by busy schedules and a lot of responsibilities. But God, in 1 Corinthians 6:19-29, reminds us that our bodies are temples of the Holy Spirit. We all belong to God, and we are called to glorify Him with our bodies. Amid the chaos, we must honor our bodies as dwelling places for God's Spirit. We must make choices that reflect His presence within us. As women of God, we must strive to seek physical health, emotional well-being, and spiritual growth. By doing so, we glorify God in all we do. Let us reflect on the sacred temples we are and commit to honoring God through self-care.

Prayer

Heavenly Father, I thank you for choosing my body to be your temple and your sacred dwelling place. I also thank you for the gift of your Holy Spirit that lives within me. I ask for your grace and help as I seek to honor you by caring for my body, which is a temple of your Presence. Dear Lord, grant me strength and wisdom for self-care and self-love. In Jesus' name, I pray. Amen.

Related Scriptures for the Week

Romans 12:1-2 (NIV):

"Therefore, I urge you, brothers and sisters, in view of God's mercy, to offer your bodies as a living sacrifice, holy and pleasing to God—this is your true and proper worship. Do not conform to the pattern of this world, but be transformed by the renewing of your mind. Then you will be able to test and approve what God's will is—his good, pleasing and perfect will."

1 Corinthians 10:31 (NIV):

"So whether you eat or drink or whatever you do, do it all for the glory of God."

Galatians 2:20 (NIV):

"I have been crucified with Christ and I no longer live, but Christ lives in me. The life I now live in the body, I live by faith in the Son of God, who loved me and gave himself for me."

1 Peter 1:15-16 (NIV):

"But just as he who called you is holy, so be holy in all you do; for it is written: 'Be holy because I am holy.'"

1 Thessalonians 4:3-4 (NIV):

"It is God's will that you should be sanctified: that you should avoid sexual immorality; that each of you should learn to control your own body in a way that is holy and honorable."

1 Corinthians 10:23 (NIV):

"I have the right to do anything, you say — but not everything is beneficial. I have the right to do anything — but not everything is constructive."

Prayer Tracker

WEEK OF: / /

PRAYER REQUEST	S	M	T	W	T	F	S
_____	○	○	○	○	○	○	○
_____	○	○	○	○	○	○	○
_____	○	○	○	○	○	○	○
_____	○	○	○	○	○	○	○
_____	○	○	○	○	○	○	○
_____	○	○	○	○	○	○	○
_____	○	○	○	○	○	○	○
_____	○	○	○	○	○	○	○
_____	○	○	○	○	○	○	○
_____	○	○	○	○	○	○	○
_____	○	○	○	○	○	○	○
_____	○	○	○	○	○	○	○
_____	○	○	○	○	○	○	○

NOTES

_____

_____

_____

_____

_____

_____

_____

Week 13: Self-Care

"For you created my inmost being; you knit me together in my mother's womb. I praise you because I am fearfully and wonderfully made; your works are wonderful; I know that full well."

Psalm 139:13-14 (NIV)

Life's pressures and demands can make us forget about how valuable and honorable we are in God's sight. God created us in His image and likeness and made us the most attractive of all created beings. How often do we take a moment to admire the beauty that God has given us? Psalms 139:13-14 remind us to give thanks to God for creating us fearfully and wonderfully. In the busyness of life, take a moment to appreciate the masterpiece you are. Embrace self-care as a means of honoring the beauty and awesomeness that God bestowed on you. May our acts of self-care show true gratitude to God.

Prayer

Wonderful God, my heart overflows with praise and gratitude for the awesome work that you did while forming every part of my body. I praise you, Lord, for fearfully and wonderfully making me in your image and likeness. God help me appreciate my unique design and practice self-care as an act of gratitude for your craftsmanship. In Jesus' name, I pray. Amen.

Related Scriptures for the Week

Jeremiah 1:5 (NIV):

"Before I formed you in the womb I knew you, before you were born I set you apart; I appointed you as a prophet to the nations."

Isaiah 44:24 (NIV):

"This is what the Lord says—your Redeemer, who formed you in the womb: I am the Lord, the Maker of all things, who stretches out the heavens, who spreads out the earth by myself."

Psalm 22:10 (NIV):

"From birth I was cast on you; from my mother's womb you have been my God."

Isaiah 49:15 (NIV):

"Can a mother forget the baby at her breast and have no compassion on the child she has borne? Though she may forget, I will not forget you!"

Job 31:15 (NIV):

"Did not he who made me in the womb make them? Did not the same one form us both within our mothers?"

Psalm 71:6 (NIV):

"From birth I have relied on you; you brought me forth from my mother's womb. I will ever praise you."

Galatians 1:15 (NIV):

"But when God, who set me apart from my mother's womb and called me by his grace, was pleased."

Psalm 22:9-10 (NIV):

"Yet you brought me out of the womb; you made me trust in you, even at my mother's breast. From birth I was cast on you; from my mother's womb you have been my God."

Prayer Tracker

WEEK OF: / /

PRAYER REQUEST	S	M	T	W	T	F	S
_____	⚪	⚪	⚪	⚪	⚪	⚪	⚪
_____	⚪	⚪	⚪	⚪	⚪	⚪	⚪
_____	⚪	⚪	⚪	⚪	⚪	⚪	⚪
_____	⚪	⚪	⚪	⚪	⚪	⚪	⚪
_____	⚪	⚪	⚪	⚪	⚪	⚪	⚪
_____	⚪	⚪	⚪	⚪	⚪	⚪	⚪
_____	⚪	⚪	⚪	⚪	⚪	⚪	⚪
_____	⚪	⚪	⚪	⚪	⚪	⚪	⚪
_____	⚪	⚪	⚪	⚪	⚪	⚪	⚪
_____	⚪	⚪	⚪	⚪	⚪	⚪	⚪
_____	⚪	⚪	⚪	⚪	⚪	⚪	⚪
_____	⚪	⚪	⚪	⚪	⚪	⚪	⚪
_____	⚪	⚪	⚪	⚪	⚪	⚪	⚪

NOTES

_____

_____

_____

_____

_____

_____

_____

Week 14: Self-Care

"Come to me, all you who are weary and burdened, and I will give you rest. Take my yoke upon you and learn from me, for I am gentle and humble in heart, and you will find rest for your souls. For my yoke is easy and my burden is light."

Matthew 11:28-30 (NIV)

Most times we carry burdens that we are not supposed to carry. We get overwhelmed by the weight of struggles that are meant to be solved by Jesus and not us. And when we do this, exhaustion can take hold. As we navigate through different life issues, we must remember Jesus' invitation to find rest in Him. Amid our busy schedules, let's heed His call to come to Him for rest. Embrace His gentleness and humility. Seek the face of the One who offers a light burden and easy yoke every morning. Through self-care practices like meditation, prayer, and stillness, you can find rest for your body and soul.

Prayer

Heavenly Father, I come to you with a heart that is weary and heavy. I thank you for offering rest and calm for my burdened soul and my tired body. Help me embrace your gentleness and prioritize self-care to find true rest in you. I lay all my worries, fears, burdens, and uncertainties at your feet as I seek to find everlasting rest and peace that surpasses all understanding. In Jesus' name, I pray. Amen!

Related Scriptures for the Week

Psalm 55:22 (NIV):

"Cast your cares on the Lord and he will sustain you; he will never let the righteous be shaken."

Isaiah 40:29-31 (NIV):

"He gives strength to the weary and increases the power of the weak. Even youths grow tired and weary, and young men stumble and fall; but those who hope in the Lord will renew their strength. They will soar on wings like eagles; they will run and not grow weary, they will walk and not be faint."

Psalm 62:1 (NIV):

"Truly my soul finds rest in God; my salvation comes from him."

1 Peter 5:7 (NIV):

"Cast all your anxiety on him because he cares for you."

Isaiah 30:15 (NIV):

"This is what the Sovereign Lord, the Holy One of Israel, says: 'In repentance and rest is your salvation, in quietness and trust is your strength, but you would have none of it.'"

Psalm 23:1-3 (NIV):

"The Lord is my shepherd, I lack nothing. He makes me lie down in green pastures, he leads me beside quiet waters, he refreshes my soul. He guides me along the right paths for his name's sake."

Psalm 116:7 (NIV):

"Return to your rest, my soul, for the Lord has been good to you."

Hebrews 4:9-10 (NIV):

"There remains, then, a Sabbath rest for the people of God; for anyone who enters God's rest also rests from their works, just as God did from his."

Prayer Tracker

WEEK OF: / /

PRAYER REQUEST

	S	M	T	W	T	F	S
_____	●	●	●	●	●	●	●
_____	●	●	●	●	●	●	●
_____	●	●	●	●	●	●	●
_____	●	●	●	●	●	●	●
_____	●	●	●	●	●	●	●
_____	●	●	●	●	●	●	●
_____	●	●	●	●	●	●	●
_____	●	●	●	●	●	●	●
_____	●	●	●	●	●	●	●
_____	●	●	●	●	●	●	●
_____	●	●	●	●	●	●	●
_____	●	●	●	●	●	●	●
_____	●	●	●	●	●	●	●

NOTES

_____

_____

_____

_____

_____

_____

_____

Week 15: Faith

"Therefore, I tell you, whatever you ask for in prayer,
believe that you have received it, and it will be yours."

Mark 11:24 (NIV)

Sometimes people lose the zeal to pray because they
don't believe that God can faithfully answer their
prayers. Other times we feel like what we want to ask
God for is too much. During such times, we forget that
God is a God of impossibilities and nothing is too hard
for Him. We may be going through situations that may
seem impossible in our eyes, but that doesn't mean that
God cannot handle them. In the midst of life's chaos,
prayer becomes our sanctuary. And as we pray, we must
approach God with unwavering faith and believe that
He hears and answers. Let our faith be the foundation
of our petitions. Amidst life's hectic pace, may we
always remember that our prayers are powerful and that
God is faithful enough to respond.

Prayer

Heavenly Father, I praise you because you are faithful to fail me. I thank you for your faithfulness over my life and for the assurance that when I call upon you, you will listen and you will answer! Help me approach you with unwavering faith every time I come before you in prayer and to trust that your answers are on the way. I ask that you strengthen my belief in your goodness. In Jesus' name, I pray. Amen.

Related Scriptures for the Week

Matthew 21:22 (NIV):

"If you believe, you will receive whatever you ask for in prayer."

James 1:6-7 (NIV):

"But when you ask, you must believe and not doubt, because the one who doubts is like a wave of the sea, blown and tossed by the wind. That person should not expect to receive anything from the Lord."

Matthew 18:19-20 (NIV):

"Again, truly I tell you that if two of you on earth agree about anything they ask for, it will be done for them by my Father in heaven. For where two or three gather in my name, there am I with them."

1 John 5:14-15 (NIV):

"This is the confidence we have in approaching God: that if we ask anything according to his will, he hears us. And if we know that he hears us—whatever we ask—we know that we have what we asked of him."

Philippians 4:6-7 (NIV):

"Do not be anxious about anything, but in every situation, by prayer and petition, with thanksgiving, present your requests to God. And the peace of God, which transcends all understanding, will guard your hearts and your minds in Christ Jesus."

John 15:7 (NIV):

"If you remain in me and my words remain in you, ask whatever you wish, and it will be done for you."

Jeremiah 29:12 (NIV):

"Then you will call on me and come and pray to me,
and I will listen to you."

1 Thessalonians 5:17 (NIV):

"Pray continually."

Prayer Tracker

WEEK OF: / /

PRAYER REQUEST	S	M	T	W	T	F	S
_____	○	○	○	○	○	○	○
_____	○	○	○	○	○	○	○
_____	○	○	○	○	○	○	○
_____	○	○	○	○	○	○	○
_____	○	○	○	○	○	○	○
_____	○	○	○	○	○	○	○
_____	○	○	○	○	○	○	○
_____	○	○	○	○	○	○	○
_____	○	○	○	○	○	○	○
_____	○	○	○	○	○	○	○
_____	○	○	○	○	○	○	○
_____	○	○	○	○	○	○	○
_____	○	○	○	○	○	○	○

NOTES

_____

_____

_____

_____

_____

_____

_____

Week 16: Faith

"Trust in the Lord with all your heart and lean not on your own understanding; in all your ways submit to Him, and He will make your paths straight."

Proverbs 3:5-6 (NIV)

When life gets hectic, we may be tempted to rely on our own understanding. We may struggle to find the fastest solutions to our problems or the easiest way out. But we end up failing because some things are beyond our control. Proverbs 3:5-6 encourage us to trust in the Lord wholeheartedly. Through the chaos of life, we must learn to surrender control to God. When you trust His ways above your own, He will guide you through the busiest of days and the most uncertain of times, and He will make your path straight. He will make a way where there seems to be no way and make what seems impossible come to pass.

Prayer

Dear Lord, I praise you because you are mighty and all-powerful. Nothing is beyond your ability, and you know the best solution to my struggles. Today, I surrender my understanding and trust in your ways. I pray that you may guide me through life's pressures and make my paths straight. Go before me, dear Lord, and straighten all crooked ways. May my trust in you grow stronger every day. In Jesus' name, I pray. Amen.

Related Scriptures for the Week

Psalm 37:3-5 (NIV):

"Trust in the Lord and do good; dwell in the land and enjoy safe pasture. Take delight in the Lord, and he will give you the desires of your heart. Commit your way to the Lord; trust in him, and he will do this."

Isaiah 26:4 (NIV):

"Trust in the Lord forever, for the Lord, the Lord himself, is the Rock eternal."

Proverbs 16:3 (NIV):

"Commit to the Lord whatever you do, and he will establish your plans."

Psalm 62:8 (NIV):

"Trust in him at all times, you people; pour out your hearts to him, for God is our refuge."

Psalm 56:3 (NIV):

"When I am afraid, I put my trust in you."

Isaiah 40:31 (NIV):

"But those who hope in the Lord will renew their strength. They will soar on wings like eagles; they will run and not grow weary, they will walk and not be faint."

Psalm 143:8 (NIV):

"Let the morning bring me word of your unfailing love, for I have put my trust in you. Show me the way I should go, for to you I entrust my life."

Hebrews 13:6 (NIV):

"So we say with confidence, 'The Lord is my helper; I will not be afraid. What can mere mortals do to me?"

Prayer Tracker

WEEK OF: / /

PRAYER REQUEST	S	M	T	W	T	F	S
_____	○	○	○	○	○	○	○
_____	○	○	○	○	○	○	○
_____	○	○	○	○	○	○	○
_____	○	○	○	○	○	○	○
_____	○	○	○	○	○	○	○
_____	○	○	○	○	○	○	○
_____	○	○	○	○	○	○	○
_____	○	○	○	○	○	○	○
_____	○	○	○	○	○	○	○
_____	○	○	○	○	○	○	○
_____	○	○	○	○	○	○	○
_____	○	○	○	○	○	○	○
_____	○	○	○	○	○	○	○

NOTES

_____

_____

_____

_____

_____

_____

_____

Week 17: Faith

"If you can?" said Jesus. "Everything is possible for
one who believes."

Mark 9:23 (NIV)

Amid the challenges that surround our lives, having
faith in God's power can transform the impossible into
reality. When faced with overwhelming situations, we
must remember that we have a God who is ready to do
anything for us as long as we put our faith in Him. Mark
9:23 tells us that all things are possible, regardless of
our age, race, or circumstance, when we believe in God.
Therefore, let faith ignite our determination and hope.
Let us train ourselves to trust that God can make a way
and grant us peace, even in the chaos.

Prayer

Heavenly Father, I come before you today acknowledging the boundless power of believing in you! I choose to trust you because I believe in the truth of your Word in Mark 9:23. Strengthen my faith in you, dear Lord, and help me see the possibilities amidst life's challenges. I believe that with you, all things are possible. In Jesus' name, I pray. Amen.

Related Scriptures for the Week

Mark 10:27 (NIV):

"Jesus looked at them and said, 'With man this is impossible, but not with God; all things are possible with God.'"

Matthew 17:20 (NIV):

"He replied, 'Because you have so little faith. Truly I tell you, if you have faith as small as a mustard seed, you can say to this mountain, "Move from here to there," and it will move. Nothing will be impossible for you.'"

Philippians 4:13 (NIV):

"I can do all this through him who gives me strength."

Jeremiah 32:27 (NIV):

"I am the Lord, the God of all mankind. Is anything too hard for me?"

Hebrews 11:6 (NIV):

"And without faith it is impossible to please God because anyone who comes to him must believe that he exists and that he rewards those who earnestly seek him."

Ephesians 3:20 (NIV):

"Now to him who is able to do immeasurably more than all we ask or imagine, according to his power that is at work within us."

Prayer Tracker

WEEK OF: / /

PRAYER REQUEST	S	M	T	W	T	F	S
	●	●	●	●	●	●	●
	●	●	●	●	●	●	●
	●	●	●	●	●	●	●
	●	●	●	●	●	●	●
	●	●	●	●	●	●	●
	●	●	●	●	●	●	●
	●	●	●	●	●	●	●
	●	●	●	●	●	●	●
	●	●	●	●	●	●	●
	●	●	●	●	●	●	●
	●	●	●	●	●	●	●
	●	●	●	●	●	●	●
	●	●	●	●	●	●	●

NOTES

Week 18: Faith

"For nothing will be impossible with God."

Luke 1:37 (NIV)

Life's demands can make us feel so limited that we may think that other things will never work out for us. The devil may take advantage of every situation to make us doubt the sovereignty of God. We may develop fear, worry, anxiety, and doubt when we are faced with endless struggles. But Luke 1:37 reminds us that with God by our side, nothing is impossible. He is God in good times and in bad times. He has the answers to our challenges and knows how to work even the most complex issues out. Amid our hectic schedule and sometimes chaotic lives, we are called to hold onto this truth. We are called to trust that God can turn the impossible into reality. Let our faith in Him empower us to face life's challenges with confidence, knowing that His power is limitless. Nothing is beyond the reach of our Almighty God.

Prayer

God, you are so powerful, and I praise you for your glory! I praise you for being able to do all things under the sun, including the things that seem impossible! I acknowledge your ability to work out all things not by power nor might, but by your powerful Spirit. I welcome you to live in my heart, and I declare that with you by my side, nothing will be impossible. Strengthen my faith to face life's challenges and impossibilities. May your Spirit help me to always trust in your limitless power. In Jesus' name, I pray. Amen.

Related Scriptures for the Week

Matthew 19:26 (NIV):

"Jesus looked at them and said, 'With man this is impossible, but with God all things are possible.'"

Jeremiah 32:17 (NIV):

"Ah, Sovereign Lord, you have made the heavens and the earth by your great power and outstretched arm. Nothing is too hard for you."

Genesis 18:14 (NIV):

"Is anything too hard for the Lord? I will return to you at the appointed time next year, and Sarah will have a son."

Job 42:2 (NIV):

"I know that you can do all things; no purpose of yours can be thwarted."

Romans 8:31 (NIV):

"What, then, shall we say in response to these things? If God is for us, who can be against us?"

Revelation 19:6 (NIV):

"Then I heard what sounded like a great multitude, like the roar of rushing waters and like loud peals of thunder, shouting: 'Hallelujah! For our Lord God Almighty reigns.'"

Prayer Tracker

WEEK OF: / /

PRAYER REQUEST	S	M	T	W	T	F	S
_____	○	○	○	○	○	○	○
_____	○	○	○	○	○	○	○
_____	○	○	○	○	○	○	○
_____	○	○	○	○	○	○	○
_____	○	○	○	○	○	○	○
_____	○	○	○	○	○	○	○
_____	○	○	○	○	○	○	○
_____	○	○	○	○	○	○	○
_____	○	○	○	○	○	○	○
_____	○	○	○	○	○	○	○
_____	○	○	○	○	○	○	○
_____	○	○	○	○	○	○	○
_____	○	○	○	○	○	○	○

NOTES

_____

_____

_____

_____

_____

_____

_____

Week 19: Faith

"So that your faith might not rest on human wisdom,
but on God's power."

1 Corinthians 2:5 (NIV)

How many times do we run to our friends, family, or mentors seeking help, guidance, and support when we are faced with life's challenges? In our busy lives, we often seek human wisdom and advice. This is good because we may get the help we need or feel a sense of comfort and support and sometimes wise counsel. But the help of mankind is not 100%; they too have their flaws, weaknesses, and biases. Their help is also limited. The only person who offers true and complete help in all aspects of our lives is God. In 1 Corinthians 2:5, God calls us to place our faith in His power and wisdom. Even when things get chaotic, we are called to remember that our faith depends on God's might, not human understanding. Let us seek His guidance, trust His wisdom, and believe in His power to guide us through any situation.

Prayer

Faithful God, today I choose to place my faith in your limitless power and divine wisdom. I repent of all the times that I put my faith in human beings, whose power and ability are limited. Forgive me Lord, and help me refocus my faith in you alone. When life's chaos and challenges arise, help me to trust your wisdom and seek your guidance. May my faith always depend on you and my heart follow your lead. In Jesus' name, I pray. Amen.

Related Scriptures for the Week

1 Corinthians 1:18 (NIV)

"For the message of the cross is foolishness to those who are perishing, but to us who are being saved it is the power of God."

1 Corinthians 1:21 (NIV)

"For since in the wisdom of God the world through its wisdom did not know him, God was pleased through the foolishness of what was preached to save those who believe."

1 Corinthians 1:25 (NIV)

"For the foolishness of God is wiser than human wisdom, and the weakness of God is stronger than human strength."

1 Corinthians 2:4 (NIV)

"My message and my preaching were not with wise and persuasive words, but with a demonstration of the Spirit's power."

2 Corinthians 5:7 (NIV)

"For we live by faith, not by sight."

Ephesians 2:8-9 (NIV)

"For it is by grace you have been saved, through faith—and this is not from yourselves, it is the gift of God—not by works, so that no one can boast."

Hebrews 11:1 (NIV)

"Now faith is confidence in what we hope for and assurance about what we do not see."

Prayer Tracker

WEEK OF: / /

PRAYER REQUEST

	S	M	T	W	T	F	S
_____	●	●	●	●	●	●	●
_____	●	●	●	●	●	●	●
_____	●	●	●	●	●	●	●
_____	●	●	●	●	●	●	●
_____	●	●	●	●	●	●	●
_____	●	●	●	●	●	●	●
_____	●	●	●	●	●	●	●
_____	●	●	●	●	●	●	●
_____	●	●	●	●	●	●	●
_____	●	●	●	●	●	●	●
_____	●	●	●	●	●	●	●
_____	●	●	●	●	●	●	●
_____	●	●	●	●	●	●	●

NOTES

_____

_____

_____

_____

_____

_____

_____

Week 20: Confidence and Identity

"But by the grace of God, I am what I am, and His grace to me was not without effect. No, I worked harder than all of them—yet not I, but the grace of God that was with me."

1 Corinthians 15:10 (NIV)

How often do we question our worth and abilities when we are going through something? We start to question our worth, our value, and our purpose. We don't believe in ourselves yet. 1 Corinthians 15:10 reminds us that our confidence is rooted in God's grace and not our own works. His grace is all powerful and empowers us to overcome the challenges of life and gives us the confidence to accomplish things we never thought we could.

Prayer

Gracious God, I thank you for your incredible grace that defines my identity. I marvel at how your grace helps me navigate through situations I never thought I could manage. Your grace empowers me to achieve things that are beyond my ability. I ask you to grant me the confidence to know and always remember that I am who I am by your grace. Help me to live out my purpose with boldness. In Jesus' name, I pray. Amen.

Related Scriptures for the Week

Ephesians 2:8-9 (NIV)

"For it is by grace you have been saved, through faith—and this is not from yourselves, it is the gift of God—not by works, so that no one can boast."

2 Corinthians 12:9 (NIV)

"But he said to me, 'My grace is sufficient for you, for my power is made perfect in weakness.' Therefore I will boast all the more gladly about my weaknesses, so that Christ's power may rest on me."

Romans 12:6-8 (NIV)

"We have different gifts, according to the grace given to each of us. If your gift is prophesying, then prophesy in accordance with your faith; if it is serving, then serve; if it is teaching, then teach; if it is to encourage, then give encouragement; if it is giving, then give generously; if it is to lead, do it diligently; if it is to show mercy, do it cheerfully."

2 Timothy 2:1 (NIV)

"You then, my son, be strong in the grace that is in Christ Jesus."

1 Peter 4:10 (NIV)

"Each of you should use whatever gift you have received to serve others, as faithful stewards of God's grace in its various forms."

Galatians 2:20 (NIV)

"I have been crucified with Christ and I no longer live, but Christ lives in me. The life I now live in the body, I live by faith in the Son of God, who loved me and gave himself for me."

Prayer Tracker

WEEK OF: / /

PRAYER REQUEST	S	M	T	W	T	F	S
_____	●	●	●	●	●	●	●
_____	●	●	●	●	●	●	●
_____	●	●	●	●	●	●	●
_____	●	●	●	●	●	●	●
_____	●	●	●	●	●	●	●
_____	●	●	●	●	●	●	●
_____	●	●	●	●	●	●	●
_____	●	●	●	●	●	●	●
_____	●	●	●	●	●	●	●
_____	●	●	●	●	●	●	●
_____	●	●	●	●	●	●	●
_____	●	●	●	●	●	●	●
_____	●	●	●	●	●	●	●

NOTES

_____

_____

_____

_____

_____

_____

_____

Week 21: Confidence and Identity

"Your beauty should not come from outward adornment, such as elaborate hairstyles and the wearing of gold jewelry or fine clothes. Rather, it should be that of your inner self, the unfading beauty of a gentle and quiet spirit, which is of great worth in God's sight."

1 Peter 3:3-4 (NIV)

We spend a lot of time and money to look good! We like to have the best clothes, jewelry, bags, and shoes! In a world that puts so much emphasis on outward appearances, the scripture reminds us about the importance of inner beauty. Just as we take time and devote ourselves to working towards a beautiful outward appearance, we also have to work on our inner beauty. Our inner beauty is the spiritual aspect of our lives, and it makes us not only attractive before mankind but before God too. It involves striving to have a heart that pursues righteousness, holiness, love, humility and kindness, among other virtues. Even when we are busy, we must remember that our true beauty lies within a gentle and quiet spirit. Our worth in God's eyes surpasses any external adornment. Let this truth boost our confidence and self-worth; God looks at our hearts and not at our physical appearances.

Prayer

Heavenly Father, I thank you for reminding me about what matters most in your sight. I am glad your Spirit has reminded me today that my identity in you is not defined by outward adornment but by inner beauty. Help me find my confidence in the inner qualities that matter most to you. Fill me with your Spirit so that my spirit may reflect your beauty, Lord. From today on, I intend to work towards having a clean and beautiful heart that will bring honor and glory to your name. In Jesus' name, I pray. Amen.

Related Scriptures for the Week

Proverbs 31:30 (NIV)

"Charm is deceptive, and beauty is fleeting; but a woman who fears the Lord is to be praised."

1 Samuel 16:7 (NIV)

"But the Lord said to Samuel, 'Do not consider his appearance or his height, for I have rejected him. The Lord does not look at the things people look at. People look at the outward appearance, but the Lord looks at the heart.'"

Matthew 5:8 (NIV)

"Blessed are the pure in heart, for they will see God."

Galatians 5:22-23 (NIV)

"But the fruit of the Spirit is love, joy, peace, forbearance, kindness, goodness, faithfulness, gentleness and self-control. Against such things there is no law."

1 Timothy 2:9-10 (NIV)

"I also want the women to dress modestly, with decency and propriety, adorning themselves, not with elaborate hairstyles or gold or pearls or expensive clothes, but with good deeds, appropriate for women who profess to worship God."

Psalm 34:18 (NIV)

"The Lord is close to the brokenhearted and saves those who are crushed in spirit."

Colossians 3:12 (NIV)

"Therefore, as God's chosen people, holy and dearly loved, clothe yourselves with compassion, kindness, humility, gentleness, and patience."

1 Samuel 16:12-13 (NIV)

"So he sent for him and had him brought in. He was glowing with health and had a fine appearance and handsome features. Then the Lord said, 'Rise and anoint him; this is the one.' So Samuel took the horn of oil and anointed him in the presence of his brothers, and from that day on the Spirit of the Lord came powerfully upon David."

Prayer Tracker

WEEK OF: / /

PRAYER REQUEST

	S	M	T	W	T	F	S
_____	○	○	○	○	○	○	○
_____	○	○	○	○	○	○	○
_____	○	○	○	○	○	○	○
_____	○	○	○	○	○	○	○
_____	○	○	○	○	○	○	○
_____	○	○	○	○	○	○	○
_____	○	○	○	○	○	○	○
_____	○	○	○	○	○	○	○
_____	○	○	○	○	○	○	○
_____	○	○	○	○	○	○	○
_____	○	○	○	○	○	○	○
_____	○	○	○	○	○	○	○
_____	○	○	○	○	○	○	○

NOTES

_____

_____

_____

_____

_____

_____

_____

Week 22: Confidence and Identity

"She is clothed with strength and dignity; she can laugh at the days to come."

Proverbs 31:25 (NIV)

Life's demands can sometimes make us feel weak and uncertain. Most times, we develop the fear of the unknown and we are scared of what the future holds. Yet, God paints a picture of confidence and hope in Proverbs 31:25. He has designed us in a special way, not as women of fear, but as women who are confident about the future. In the midst of our hectic days, let us strive to clothe ourselves with strength and honor. Let us find confidence in knowing that our future is secure in God's hands. We have been fully equipped and designed by God to face whatever comes our way. When life tries to make us believe that the future is bleak, let us arise and walk as God has called us because He has clothed us with confidence, honor, and strength.

Prayer

Almighty God, I give you thanks for designing me in a special way. My soul seeks the strength, honor, and courage that come from you. Lord cover me with confidence that I may confidently face the future knowing that it is held in your loving hands. Teach me to rise with strength in every situation that comes my way and be hopeful of better days ahead of me. In Jesus' name, I pray. Amen.

Related Scriptures for the Week

Philippians 4:13 (NIV)

"I can do all things through him who gives me strength."

1 Corinthians 16:13 (NIV)

"Be on your guard; stand firm in the faith; be courageous; be strong."

Psalm 27:1 (NIV)

"The Lord is my light and my salvation—whom shall I fear? The Lord is the stronghold of my life—of whom shall I be afraid?"

Isaiah 40:31 (NIV)

"But those who hope in the Lord will renew their strength. They will soar on wings like eagles; they will run and not grow weary, they will walk and not be faint.

2 Timothy 1:7 (NIV)

"For the Spirit God gave us does not make us timid, but gives us power, love, and self-discipline."

Psalm 112:7 (NIV)

"They will have no fear of bad news; their hearts are steadfast, trusting in the Lord."

Psalm 31:24 (NIV)

"Be strong and take heart, all you who hope in the Lord."

Prayer Tracker

WEEK OF: / /

PRAYER REQUEST	S	M	T	W	T	F	S
_____	○	○	○	○	○	○	○
_____	○	○	○	○	○	○	○
_____	○	○	○	○	○	○	○
_____	○	○	○	○	○	○	○
_____	○	○	○	○	○	○	○
_____	○	○	○	○	○	○	○
_____	○	○	○	○	○	○	○
_____	○	○	○	○	○	○	○
_____	○	○	○	○	○	○	○
_____	○	○	○	○	○	○	○
_____	○	○	○	○	○	○	○
_____	○	○	○	○	○	○	○
_____	○	○	○	○	○	○	○

NOTES

_____

_____

_____

_____

_____

_____

Week 23: Confidence and Identity

"For I know the plans I have for you," declares the Lord, "plans to prosper you and not to harm you, plans to give you hope and a future."

Jeremiah 29:11 (NIV)

When troubles arise and challenges come our way, we often question our future and purpose. We wonder whether our plans and dreams will ever come to fruition. However, this verse reminds us that God has plans filled with hope for us. He knows what our future holds and wants us to believe and align our thoughts with His perfect plan. With everything going on in life, we must trust in God's purpose for our lives. Our identity is rooted in His plans, which bring peace, hope, and better days. Let us find confidence in His guidance for our future. Let us position our hearts to embrace God's plans with confidence and hope.

Prayer

Heavenly Father, I praise you because you are faithful, kind, and compassionate towards me. My heart overflows with gratitude for the hope-filled plans you have for my life. As I come before you today, I pray that you may help me find confidence in your purpose and trust your guidance for the future. I don't want to ever grow anxious or uncertain about what my future holds because I know it is in the best hands– your hands. May my heart always be at peace in the knowledge of this truth. In Jesus' name, I pray. Amen.

Related Scriptures for the Week

Proverbs 3:5-6 (NIV)

"Trust in the Lord with all your heart and lean not on your own understanding; in all your ways submit to him, and he will make your paths straight."

Isaiah 55:8-9 (NIV)

"For my thoughts are not your thoughts, neither are your ways my ways, declares the Lord. As the heavens are higher than the earth, so are my ways higher than your ways and my thoughts than your thoughts."

Jeremiah 29:12-13 (NIV)

"Then you will call on me and come and pray to me, and I will listen to you. You will seek me and find me when you seek me with all your heart."

Romans 8:28 (NIV)

"And we know that in all things God works for the good of those who love him, who have been called according to his purpose."

Psalm 37:4 (NIV)

"Take delight in the Lord, and he will give you the desires of your heart."

Psalm 130:5 (NIV)

"I wait for the Lord, my whole being waits, and in his word I put my hope."

Proverbs 16:9 (NIV)

"In their hearts humans plan their course, but the
Lord establishes their steps."

Lamentations 3:25 (NIV)

"The Lord is good to those whose hope is in him, to
the one who seeks him."

Prayer Tracker

WEEK OF: / /

PRAYER REQUEST   S   M   T   W   T   F   S

_____

_____

_____

_____

_____

_____

_____

_____

_____

_____

_____

_____

_____

NOTES

_____

_____

_____

_____

_____

_____

_____

Week 24: Confidence and Identity

"But you are a chosen people, a royal priesthood, a holy nation, God's special possession, that you may declare the praises of Him who called you out of darkness into His wonderful light."

1 Peter 2:9 (NIV)

Whenever we feel like we are not valuable or important in the society we live in, we must remember that we were chosen long ago by God to be His people and we are precious in His sight. No amount of challenges, struggles, or weaknesses can change this fact. God knew our strengths, weaknesses, and failures, and He still chose us! Even on your busy days, remember to cling to your identity as God's chosen one even when you feel like you are too weak to accomplish anything. You are part of a royal priesthood, a holy nation, and a people that is very important before the Lord. Your purpose is to declare His praises and not to feel out of place. Find confidence in being called out of darkness into His wonderful light. Let us strive to always walk in the confidence of our chosen and precious identities.

Prayer

Dear Lord, I come before you today to specifically thank you for choosing me. I find my confidence in being chosen by you, the Creator of Heaven and Earth. Help me declare your praises with joy. Amid the struggles, doubts, and fears that engulf my life, I will praise you, O Lord, for you have given me a special identity in your love and grace. May I always shine brightly in your wonderful light and may my life reflect my identity as your special possession. In Jesus' name, I pray. Amen.

Related Scriptures for the Week
Exodus 19:6 (NIV)

"You will be for me a kingdom of priests and a holy nation. These are the words you are to speak to the Israelites."

Revelation 1:6 (NIV)

"and has made us to be a kingdom and priests to serve his God and Father—to him be glory and power for ever and ever! Amen."

1 Peter 2:5 (NIV)

"you also, like living stones, are being built into a spiritual house to be a holy priesthood, offering spiritual sacrifices acceptable to God through Jesus Christ."

Revelation 5:10 (NIV)

"You have made them to be a kingdom and priests to serve our God, and they will reign on the earth."

Hebrews 13:15 (NIV)

"Through Jesus, therefore, let us continually offer to God a sacrifice of praise—the fruit of lips that openly profess his name."

Psalm 107:1 (NIV)

"Give thanks to the Lord, for he is good; his love endures forever."

1 Chronicles 16:24 (NIV)

"Declare his glory among the nations, his marvelous deeds among all peoples."

1 Thessalonians 5:9-10 (NIV)

"For God did not appoint us to suffer wrath but to receive salvation through our Lord Jesus Christ. He died for us so that, whether we are awake or asleep, we may live together with him."

Prayer Tracker

WEEK OF: / /

PRAYER REQUEST	S	M	T	W	T	F	S
_____	○	○	○	○	○	○	○
_____	○	○	○	○	○	○	○
_____	○	○	○	○	○	○	○
_____	○	○	○	○	○	○	○
_____	○	○	○	○	○	○	○
_____	○	○	○	○	○	○	○
_____	○	○	○	○	○	○	○
_____	○	○	○	○	○	○	○
_____	○	○	○	○	○	○	○
_____	○	○	○	○	○	○	○
_____	○	○	○	○	○	○	○
_____	○	○	○	○	○	○	○
_____	○	○	○	○	○	○	○

NOTES

_____

_____

_____

_____

_____

_____

_____

Week 25: Friendship and Community

"One who has unreliable friends soon comes to ruin, but there is a friend who sticks closer than a brother."

Proverbs 18:24 (NIV)

We all have that one friend who stands by us when things are working out well and when they aren't. Such types of friends are rare, and if we are privileged to have one, we should appreciate their presence in our lives. In a world of uncertainty and chaos, the importance of true friendship and a reliable community becomes clear. Friends and the community that surrounds us can play a very significant role in shaping our lives and providing unwavering support. In the busyness of our days, we must remember to cherish those who are genuine friends, for they are a gift from God. What are we doing to maintain our good relationships with our friends? Do we pray for them? Do we check on them randomly? Do we offer words of encouragement? Even when we are really busy, it's important to try to be there for our friends. Remember the words of Proverbs 18:24: 'A friend can stick closer than a brother.' Therefore, let us appreciate their presence in our lives.

Prayer

Heavenly Father, I thank you for the gift of genuine friendships and the reliable community that surrounds me. I thank you for each of their lives and for the roles they play in my life. Lord, I ask you to bless them and meet every other desire of their hearts. Help me cherish and nurture these relationships amidst my busy lifestyle. I pray that I may be a true friend to them as well; a friend they can count on in their times of joy and times of need. May our friendship reflect your love, kindness, and faithfulness. In Jesus' name, I pray. Amen.

Related Scriptures for the Week

Proverbs 17:17 (NIV)

"A friend loves at all times, and a brother is born for a time of adversity."

Ecclesiastes 4:9-10 (NIV)

"Two are better than one because they have a good return for their labor: If either of them falls down, one can help the other up. But pity anyone who falls and has no one to help them up."

John 15:13 (NIV)

"Greater love has no one than this: to lay down one's life for one's friends."

Proverbs 27:9 (NIV)

"Perfume and incense bring joy to the heart, and the pleasantness of a friend springs from their heartfelt advice."

1 Samuel 18:1 (NIV)

"After David had finished talking with Saul, Jonathan became one in spirit with David, and he loved him as himself."

Proverbs 27:6 (NIV)

"Wounds from a friend can be trusted, but an enemy multiplies kisses."

James 2:23 (NIV)

"And the scripture was fulfilled that says, 'Abraham believed God, and it was credited to him as righteousness,' and he was called God's friend."

1 Corinthians 15:33 (NIV)

"Do not be misled: 'Bad company corrupts good character.'"

Prayer Tracker

WEEK OF: / /

PRAYER REQUEST	S	M	T	W	T	F	S
_____	○	○	○	○	○	○	○
_____	○	○	○	○	○	○	○
_____	○	○	○	○	○	○	○
_____	○	○	○	○	○	○	○
_____	○	○	○	○	○	○	○
_____	○	○	○	○	○	○	○
_____	○	○	○	○	○	○	○
_____	○	○	○	○	○	○	○
_____	○	○	○	○	○	○	○
_____	○	○	○	○	○	○	○
_____	○	○	○	○	○	○	○
_____	○	○	○	○	○	○	○
_____	○	○	○	○	○	○	○

NOTES

_____

_____

_____

_____

_____

_____

_____

Week 26: Friendship and Community

"A new command I give you: Love one another. As I
have loved you, so you must love one another. By this,
everyone will know that you are my disciples if you
love one another.

John 13:34-35 (NIV)

Love is not just an emotion that we feel towards the
people we cherish but a command from God. God
commands us to love one another regardless of whether
they are close to us or not. The love we show towards
others does not only reflect our affection towards them
but proves to the world that we are daughters of God.
Our love for others reflects our identity as followers of
Christ. Amidst our busy schedules, we must prioritize
love in all our interactions. It is important to remember
that not everyone will reciprocate the love we show them.
But this should not stop us from being compassionate
towards them. Let your love for others be a testimony to

your faith and obedience to the command of God. In loving one another as Christ loves us, we bear witness to His presence in our lives.

Prayer

Compassionate God, I thank you for your unconditional love. I acknowledge your love that has no end. Thank you for the command to love one another in the same way that you have shown immense love towards me. I pray that you may help me to embody this love in my daily interactions and to show others the beauty of your grace. I desire that everyone who interacts with me experiences your love and kindness through me. Grant me the grace to live in obedience to your command in the scripture. In Jesus' name, I pray. Amen.

Related Scriptures for the Week

1 John 4:7 (NIV)

"Dear friends, let us love one another, for love comes from God. Everyone who loves has been born of God and knows God."

1 John 4:11 (NIV)

"Dear friends, since God so loved us, we also ought to love one another."

Colossians 3:14 (NIV)

"And over all these virtues put on love, which binds them all together in perfect unity."

Romans 13:8 (NIV)

"Let no debt remain outstanding, except the continuing debt to love one another, for whoever loves others has fulfilled the law."

Galatians 5:13 (NIV)

"You, my brothers and sisters, were called to be free. But do not use your freedom to indulge the flesh; rather, serve one another humbly in love."

1 Thessalonians 4:9 (NIV)

"Now about your love for one another we do not need to write to you, for you yourselves have been taught by God to love each other."

1 Corinthians 16:14 (NIV)

"Do everything in love."

Prayer Tracker

WEEK OF: / /

PRAYER REQUEST	S	M	T	W	T	F	S
_____	●	●	●	●	●	●	●
_____	●	●	●	●	●	●	●
_____	●	●	●	●	●	●	●
_____	●	●	●	●	●	●	●
_____	●	●	●	●	●	●	●
_____	●	●	●	●	●	●	●
_____	●	●	●	●	●	●	●
_____	●	●	●	●	●	●	●
_____	●	●	●	●	●	●	●
_____	●	●	●	●	●	●	●
_____	●	●	●	●	●	●	●
_____	●	●	●	●	●	●	●
_____	●	●	●	●	●	●	●

NOTES

_____

_____

_____

_____

_____

_____

_____

Week 27: Friendships and Community

"Be devoted to one another in love. Honor one another above yourselves."

Romans 12:10 (NIV)

The bible calls us to friendships and community with a love that transcends the ordinary. Amid our busy lifestyles we are challenged to devote genuine and sacrificial love to one another. To honor someone above ourselves requires humility, patience, and a willingness to see the beauty in others. As we navigate the busyness of life, let this love be the guiding force in our interactions. And as we create time to fulfill our responsibilities and purpose, let us also create time to foster healthy relationships. May we see to it that our friendships and interactions bring glory and honor to the Lord.

Prayer

Gracious Father, we humbly ask you to empower us to embody the love and honor described in Romans 12:10. Help us, God, to devote ourselves to one another in a way that mirrors your sacrificial love for us. We pray that you grant us the humility to honor others above ourselves, even in the rush of our daily lives. As we navigate friendships and community, let your love be the foundation that strengthens and sustains us. In the name of Jesus, we pray. Amen.

Related Scriptures for the Week

Romans 13:7 (NIV)

"Give to everyone what you owe them: If you owe taxes, pay taxes; if revenue, then revenue; if respect, then respect; if honor, then honor."

1 Peter 5:5 (NIV)

"In the same way, you who are younger, submit yourselves to your elders. All of you, clothe yourselves with humility toward one another because, 'God opposes the proud but shows favor to the humble.'"

Philippians 2:3 (NIV)

"Do nothing out of selfish ambition or vain conceit. Rather, in humility value others above yourselves."

1 Corinthians 10:24 (NIV)

"No one should seek their own good, but the good of others."

Hebrews 13:1-2 (NIV)

"Let mutual love continue. Do not neglect to show hospitality to strangers, for thereby some have entertained angels unawares."

1 Thessalonians 5:11 (NIV)

"Therefore encourage one another and build each other up, just as in fact you are doing."

Ephesians 4:2 (NIV)

"Be completely humble and gentle; be patient, bearing with one another in love."

Prayer Tracker

WEEK OF: / /

PRAYER REQUEST	S	M	T	W	T	F	S
_____	○	○	○	○	○	○	○
_____	○	○	○	○	○	○	○
_____	○	○	○	○	○	○	○
_____	○	○	○	○	○	○	○
_____	○	○	○	○	○	○	○
_____	○	○	○	○	○	○	○
_____	○	○	○	○	○	○	○
_____	○	○	○	○	○	○	○
_____	○	○	○	○	○	○	○
_____	○	○	○	○	○	○	○
_____	○	○	○	○	○	○	○
_____	○	○	○	○	○	○	○
_____	○	○	○	○	○	○	○

NOTES

_____

_____

_____

_____

_____

_____

_____

Week 28: Friendships and Community

"Fools show their annoyance at once, but the prudent overlook an insult."

Proverbs 12:16 (NIV)

Friendships and community are not without challenges. Sometimes we encounter tricky situations or misunderstandings. But even when we are busy, we must find time to mend our relationships and restore the bond between us and our loved ones. When someone gets on our nerves, our first instinct might be to let them know right away. But Proverbs suggests a different approach— it encourages us not to react quickly to annoyances but to be patient and to let go of small hurts. Even when things are so busy we can not see straight, we are called to be calm friends (or family) who do not let things bother them too much. So, let's strive to be patient and understanding when faced with irritating moments.

Prayer

Dear God, thank you for the wisdom you provide for our relationships in Proverbs 12:16. We call upon you to help us be patient when annoyances come our way. Lord, we pray for the wisdom to solve little misunderstandings without having angry outbursts. Guide us to overlook small hurts and not react too quickly. In the hustle of our days, we pray that your wisdom be the calming presence that shapes our responses with understanding and grace. May our interactions reflect your peace and patience. In the name of Jesus! Amen.

Related Scriptures for the Week

Proverbs 13:20 (NIV)

"Walk with the wise and become wise, for a companion of fools suffers harm."

1 Corinthians 15:33 (NIV)"

Do not be misled: 'Bad company corrupts good character.'"

Proverbs 22:24-25 (NIV)

"Do not make friends with a hot-tempered person, do not associate with one easily angered, or you may learn their ways and get yourself ensnared."

Psalm 1:1-2 (NIV)

"Blessed is the one who does not walk in step with the wicked or stand in the way that sinners take or sit in the company of mockers, but whose delight is in the law of the Lord, and who meditates on his law day and night."

2 Corinthians 6:14 (NIV)

"Do not be yoked together with unbelievers. For what do righteousness and wickedness have in common? Or what fellowship can light have with darkness?"

Proverbs 14:7 (NIV)

"Stay away from a fool, for you will not find knowledge on their lips."

James 4:4 (NIV)

"You adulterous people, don't you know that friendship with the world means enmity against God? Therefore, anyone who chooses to be a friend of the world becomes an enemy of God."

Proverbs 27:17 (NIV)

"As iron sharpens iron, so one person sharpens another."

Prayer Tracker

WEEK OF: / /

PRAYER REQUEST

	S	M	T	W	T	F	S
_____	●	●	●	●	●	●	●
_____	●	●	●	●	●	●	●
_____	●	●	●	●	●	●	●
_____	●	●	●	●	●	●	●
_____	●	●	●	●	●	●	●
_____	●	●	●	●	●	●	●
_____	●	●	●	●	●	●	●
_____	●	●	●	●	●	●	●
_____	●	●	●	●	●	●	●
_____	●	●	●	●	●	●	●
_____	●	●	●	●	●	●	●
_____	●	●	●	●	●	●	●
_____	●	●	●	●	●	●	●

NOTES

_____

_____

_____

_____

_____

_____

_____

Week 29: Friendships and Community

"Anyone who withholds kindness from a friend
forsakes the fear of the Almighty."

Job 6:14 (NIV)

Real relationships, real friendships, and divine community are created by God. Therefore, we must maintain them with the virtues that reflect God's heart. In Job 6:14, Job is saying that when we choose not to be kind to our friends, it's like forgetting to respect and honor God. In the Bible, everyone who had an encounter with Jesus experienced His love and kindness. And as women of God, this is what God desires from us. When we have so much going on, it's easy to overlook the power of small acts of kindness. But this verse reminds us that when we show kindness to our friends, we are not just being nice to them; rather, we are honoring God. So, let's make an effort to sprinkle kindness into our friendships.

Prayer

Dear God, we thank you for our friendships and the supportive community around us. We lift our voices to you today to ask you to help us not to forget the importance of kindness in our friendships. Please, Lord, guide us to be intentional about showing love and respect to our friends, knowing that it reflects our reverence for you. In the midst of our busy lives, let our actions be a source of kindness that honors you. In the name of Jesus, we pray. Amen.

Related Scriptures for the Week

Proverbs 19:17 (NIV)

"Whoever is kind to the poor lends to the Lord, and he will reward them for what they have done."

Luke 6:35 (NIV)

"But love your enemies, do good to them, and lend to them without expecting to get anything back. Then your reward will be great, and you will be children of the Most High because he is kind to the ungrateful and wicked."

Galatians 6:10 (NIV)

"Therefore, as we have opportunity, let us do good to all people, especially to those who belong to the family of believers."

Ephesians 4:32 (NIV)

"Be kind and compassionate to one another, forgiving each other, just as in Christ God forgave you."

Colossians 3:12 (NIV)

"Therefore, as God's chosen people, holy and dearly loved, clothe yourselves with compassion, kindness, humility, gentleness, and patience."

Matthew 5:7 (NIV)

"Blessed are the merciful, for they will be shown mercy."

Proverbs 3:27-28 (NIV)

"Do not withhold good from those to whom it is due when it is in your power to act. Do not say to your neighbor, 'Come back tomorrow, and I'll give it to you'—when you already have it with you."

Micah 6:8 (NIV)

"He has shown you, O mortal, what is good. And what does the Lord require of you? To act justly and to love mercy and to walk humbly with your God."

Prayer Tracker

WEEK OF: / /

PRAYER REQUEST	S	M	T	W	T	F	S
_____	◯	◯	◯	◯	◯	◯	◯
_____	◯	◯	◯	◯	◯	◯	◯
_____	◯	◯	◯	◯	◯	◯	◯
_____	◯	◯	◯	◯	◯	◯	◯
_____	◯	◯	◯	◯	◯	◯	◯
_____	◯	◯	◯	◯	◯	◯	◯
_____	◯	◯	◯	◯	◯	◯	◯
_____	◯	◯	◯	◯	◯	◯	◯
_____	◯	◯	◯	◯	◯	◯	◯
_____	◯	◯	◯	◯	◯	◯	◯
_____	◯	◯	◯	◯	◯	◯	◯
_____	◯	◯	◯	◯	◯	◯	◯
_____	◯	◯	◯	◯	◯	◯	◯

NOTES

_____

_____

_____

_____

_____

_____

_____

Week 30: Stress and Pressure

"Consider it pure joy, my brothers and sisters, whenever you face trials of many kinds, because you know that the testing of your faith produces perseverance. Let perseverance finish its work so that you may be mature and complete, not lacking anything."

James 1:2-4 (NIV)

Life can sometimes feel like a storm, tossing us around with deadlines, expectations, disappointments, and difficulties. Even through all of us, the Bible calls us to find joy in these trials. This is not about pretending everything is easy but rather understanding that the trials we endure can help shape us. The challenges that come into our lives do not come to break us but to mold our character and make us stronger and more resilient. So, as we navigate the stress of our lives, let us consider each trial as an opportunity for growth and for God to perfect His work within us. Challenges can test the virtues of patience and endurance which help us wait for God's perfect timing. And as the Scripture in James 1:2-4 says, when we persevere through life's pressures, we will lack nothing at the end of it all.

Prayer

Dear God, as we face the storms of stress and pressure, help us to embrace them with joy. We humbly ask you to grant us the strength to see trials as opportunities for growth, elevation, and more grace in our lives. In the midst of life's demands, may we find resilience and perseverance, knowing that these challenges can shape us into better versions of ourselves. In the name of Jesus. Amen.

Related Scriptures for the Week
Romans 5:3-4 (NIV)

"Not only so, but we also glory in our sufferings because we know that suffering produces perseverance; perseverance, character; and character, hope."

2 Corinthians 12:9-10 (NIV)

"But he said to me, 'My grace is sufficient for you, for my power is made perfect in weakness.' Therefore, I will boast all the more gladly about my weaknesses, so that Christ's power may rest on me. That is why, for Christ's sake, I delight in weaknesses, in insults, in hardships, in persecutions, in difficulties. For when I am weak, then I am strong."

1 Peter 1:6-7 (NIV)

"In all this you greatly rejoice, though now for a little while you may have had to suffer grief in all kinds of trials. These have come so that the proven genuineness of your faith—of greater worth than gold, which perishes even though refined by fire—may result in praise, glory, and honor when Jesus Christ is revealed."

Hebrews 10:36 (NIV)

"You need to persevere so that when you have done the will of God, you will receive what he has promised."

James 5:11 (NIV)

"As you know, we count as blessed those who have persevered. You have heard of Job's perseverance and have seen what the Lord finally brought about. The Lord is full of compassion and mercy."

Psalm 34:19 (NIV)

"The righteous person may have many troubles, but the Lord delivers him from them all."

Isaiah 40:31 (NIV)

"But those who hope in the Lord will renew their strength. They will soar on wings like eagles; they will run and not grow weary, they will walk and not be faint."

Prayer Tracker

WEEK OF: / /

PRAYER REQUEST	S	M	T	W	T	F	S
_____	○	○	○	○	○	○	○
_____	○	○	○	○	○	○	○
_____	○	○	○	○	○	○	○
_____	○	○	○	○	○	○	○
_____	○	○	○	○	○	○	○
_____	○	○	○	○	○	○	○
_____	○	○	○	○	○	○	○
_____	○	○	○	○	○	○	○
_____	○	○	○	○	○	○	○
_____	○	○	○	○	○	○	○
_____	○	○	○	○	○	○	○
_____	○	○	○	○	○	○	○
_____	○	○	○	○	○	○	○

NOTES

_____

_____

_____

_____

_____

_____

_____

Week 31: Stress and Pressure

"Stand firm, and you will win life."

Luke 21:19 (NIV)

Life can often throw unexpected twists. These twists and turns test our patience and resolve. But as women of faith, we are called to stand firm and remain steadfast in God. Instead of giving in to frustration, stress, anxiety, and disappointments, Jesus encourages us to stand firm so that we may succeed and prosper in our endeavors. Patience and faith are like the anchors that help us stay strong when storms rise against us. They are our pathway to victory. Our ability to stay grounded in patience allows us to navigate the ups and downs. So, let us embrace the virtue of endurance, knowing that through patience, we find a strength that transcends life's uncertainties.

Prayer

Dear God, as we face uncertainties and disappointments in life, please do not leave us alone. Just as you promised to be with us and uphold us with your righteous right hand, we ask you to show up in every situation and uphold us in your loving embrace. Lord, we pray that you grant us the strength to stand firm with patience, as your Word teaches. Help us endure challenges with grace and resilience. May our hearts be anchored in patience and faith so that we can emerge victorious in the battles that life presents. In the name of Jesus, we pray. Amen.

Related Scriptures for the Week

1 Corinthians 15:58 (NIV)

"Therefore, my dear brothers and sisters, stand firm. Let nothing move you. Always give yourselves fully to the work of the Lord because you know that your labor in the Lord is not in vain."

Galatians 6:9 (NIV)

"Let us not become weary in doing good, for at the proper time we will reap a harvest if we do not give up."

1 Corinthians 16:13 (NIV)

"Be on your guard; stand firm in the faith; be courageous; be strong."

Ephesians 6:13 (NIV)

"Therefore put on the full armor of God so that when the day of evil comes, you may be able to stand your ground, and after you have done everything, to stand."

1 Peter 5:9 (NIV)

"Resist him, standing firm in the faith, because you know that the family of believers throughout the world is undergoing the same kind of sufferings."

Psalm 37:24 (NIV)

"though he may stumble, he will not fall, for the Lord upholds him with his hand."

Hebrews 10:23 (NIV)

"Let us hold unswervingly to the hope we profess, for he who promised is faithful."

Prayer Tracker

WEEK OF: / /

PRAYER REQUEST	S	M	T	W	T	F	S
_____	○	○	○	○	○	○	○
_____	○	○	○	○	○	○	○
_____	○	○	○	○	○	○	○
_____	○	○	○	○	○	○	○
_____	○	○	○	○	○	○	○
_____	○	○	○	○	○	○	○
_____	○	○	○	○	○	○	○
_____	○	○	○	○	○	○	○
_____	○	○	○	○	○	○	○
_____	○	○	○	○	○	○	○
_____	○	○	○	○	○	○	○
_____	○	○	○	○	○	○	○
_____	○	○	○	○	○	○	○

NOTES

_____

_____

_____

_____

_____

_____

_____

Week 32: Stress and Pressure

"Therefore do not worry about tomorrow, for tomorrow will worry about itself. Each day has enough trouble of its own."

Matthew 6:34 (NIV)

Life's demands often tempt us to worry about what's coming next. We worry about how we can become great mothers to our children, what we will feed them tomorrow and the days ahead, if our husbands and significant others are happy, what we will wear to upcoming events, how our businesses will end up, and so much more. But this verse encourages a different mindset. It instructs us to take one day at a time. Instead of letting the weight of tomorrow overwhelm us, the Bible encourages us to focus on today. By doing so, we can savor each moment and find peace in the midst of life's challenges.

Prayer

Dear God, we thank you for the grace you provide us each day. We are thankful that you always show up every single day with new love and mercy. In recognition of your love which is new every morning, we ask you to help us heed the advice in Matthew 6:34 and not worry too much about tomorrow. We believe that with tomorrow's new grace and mercy everything will be okay. Father, please grant us the strength to focus on today's challenges, knowing that each day has its own troubles. In our busy lives, may we find peace in taking one step at a time and trust that you are with us every day. In the name of Jesus, we pray. Amen.

Related Scriptures for the Week

Psalm 119:165 (NIV)

"Great peace have those who love your law, and nothing can make them stumble."

Psalm 119:50 (NIV)

"My comfort in my suffering is this: Your promise preserves my life."

Psalm 119:92 (NIV)

"If your law had not been my delight, I would have perished in my affliction."

Proverbs 3:5-6 (NIV)

"Trust in the Lord with all your heart and lean not on your own understanding; in all your ways submit to him, and he will make your paths straight."

Isaiah 26:3 (NIV)

"You will keep in perfect peace those whose minds are steadfast because they trust in you."

2 Corinthians 1:3-4 (NIV)

"Praise be to the God and Father of our Lord Jesus Christ, the Father of compassion and the God of all comfort, who comforts us in all our troubles so that we can comfort those in any trouble with the comfort we ourselves receive from God."

Psalm 34:17 (NIV)

"The righteous cry out, and the Lord hears them; he delivers them from all their troubles."

Psalm 34:18 (NIV)

"The Lord is close to the brokenhearted and saves those who are crushed in spirit."

Prayer Tracker

WEEK OF: / /

PRAYER REQUEST	S	M	T	W	T	F	S
_____	○	○	○	○	○	○	○
_____	○	○	○	○	○	○	○
_____	○	○	○	○	○	○	○
_____	○	○	○	○	○	○	○
_____	○	○	○	○	○	○	○
_____	○	○	○	○	○	○	○
_____	○	○	○	○	○	○	○
_____	○	○	○	○	○	○	○
_____	○	○	○	○	○	○	○
_____	○	○	○	○	○	○	○
_____	○	○	○	○	○	○	○
_____	○	○	○	○	○	○	○
_____	○	○	○	○	○	○	○

NOTES

_____

_____

_____

_____

_____

_____

_____

Week 33: Stress and Pressure

"Trouble and distress have come upon me, but your commands give me delight."

Psalms 119:143 (NIV)

When stress and pressure surround us, turning to God's Word becomes a source of comfort. The Word of God is full of encouraging and inspiring words that can help us find peace while dealing with the troubles of life. In the Bible, we find stories of people who overcame adversity and tribulation. Women like Hagar, who had such a hard life as an enslaved woman but God protected her and was faithful through her suffering. Women like Hannah, who thought she was barren but eventually bore many sons and daughters! And women like Ruth, who was very poor but endured the economic challenges and eventually married a kind man who provided for her. These stories inspire us to press on and keep trusting in God since He is the same God who changed their situations. While troubles may knock at our door, immerse yourself in the Word of God to find guidance and pray often to find solace.

Prayer

Heavenly Father, we thank you for your Word which has always been a source of hope and encouragement in times of distress. As we encounter trouble and distress, help us to turn to your Word for comfort and guidance. We ask, dear Lord, that you grant us the ability to find delight in your commands, even when it's hard. In our hectic lives, may your Spirit help us to create time to read and meditate on your Word. We thank you, dear Father, for all the stories of faith and for the way you helped people overcome difficult situations in the Bible. May the promises and comforting words of your Word be our companion in every situation. In Jesus' name, we pray. Amen.

Related Scriptures for the Week

Philippians 4:6-7 (NIV)

"Do not be anxious about anything, but in every situation, by prayer and petition, with thanksgiving, present your requests to God. And the peace of God, which transcends all understanding, will guard your hearts and your minds in Christ Jesus."

Psalm 34:4 (NIV)

"I sought the Lord, and he answered me; he delivered me from all my fears."

Isaiah 41:10 (NIV)

"So do not fear, for I am with you; do not be dismayed, for I am your God. I will strengthen you and help you; I will uphold you with my righteous right hand."

Luke 12:25-26 (NIV)

"Who of you by worrying can add a single hour to your life? Since you cannot do this very little thing, why do you worry about the rest?"

Psalm 94:19 (NIV)

"When anxiety was great within me, your consolation brought me joy."

Prayer Tracker

WEEK OF: / /

PRAYER REQUEST	S	M	T	W	T	F	S
_____	●	●	●	●	●	●	●
_____	●	●	●	●	●	●	●
_____	●	●	●	●	●	●	●
_____	●	●	●	●	●	●	●
_____	●	●	●	●	●	●	●
_____	●	●	●	●	●	●	●
_____	●	●	●	●	●	●	●
_____	●	●	●	●	●	●	●
_____	●	●	●	●	●	●	●
_____	●	●	●	●	●	●	●
_____	●	●	●	●	●	●	●
_____	●	●	●	●	●	●	●
_____	●	●	●	●	●	●	●

NOTES

_____

_____

_____

_____

_____

_____

_____

Week 34: Stress and Pressure

"Anxiety weighs down the heart, but a kind word cheers it up."

Proverbs 12:25 (NIV)

The issues we deal with in life can be heavy with worries that burden our hearts. However, this does not mean that we should always put on a sulky face and respond to others with harshness. If we know that we are carrying a lot in our hearts, we cannot assume that others are having it much easier. When we carry the weight of life's pressures and stresses in our hearts, we become anxious and bitter. This makes us not only harsh towards ourselves but to other people as well. However, Proverbs 12:25 introduces a remedy. It teaches us to speak kind words even when we are going through tough times. A kind word, spoken with love, has the power to lift spirits and bring warmth to a troubled heart. Let us always be mindful of the impact our words can have as we strive to choose kindness as a balm for anxiety.

Prayer

Dear God, as we navigate the anxieties of life, we pray that you instill in us the power of kind words. We acknowledge that it is not easy to be kind and friendly to others when our hearts are hurting. We call on you to send the Holy Spirit to reign in our hearts and help us reflect virtues of the fruit of the Spirit, most especially kindness, in our interactions. Please, Lord, help us to be aware of those around us who may be going through challenges as well. May our words be sources of encouragement and cheer to them. In our interactions, let kindness be a reflection of your love and grace. In the name of Jesus, we pray. Amen.

Related Scriptures for the Week

1 Peter 5:7 (NIV)

"Cast all your anxiety on him because he cares for you."

Proverbs 15:23 (NIV)

"A person finds joy in giving an apt reply—and how good is a timely word!"

Matthew 11:28-30 (NIV)

"Come to me, all you who are weary and burdened, and I will give you rest. Take my yoke upon you and learn from me, for I am gentle and humble in heart, and you will find rest for your souls. For my yoke is easy and my burden is light."

Proverbs 16:24 (NIV)

"Gracious words are a honeycomb, sweet to the soul and healing to the bones."

Psalm 55:22 (NIV)

"Cast your cares on the Lord and he will sustain you; he will never let the righteous be shaken."

Prayer Tracker

WEEK OF: / /

PRAYER REQUEST	S	M	T	W	T	F	S
_____	●	●	●	●	●	●	●
_____	●	●	●	●	●	●	●
_____	●	●	●	●	●	●	●
_____	●	●	●	●	●	●	●
_____	●	●	●	●	●	●	●
_____	●	●	●	●	●	●	●
_____	●	●	●	●	●	●	●
_____	●	●	●	●	●	●	●
_____	●	●	●	●	●	●	●
_____	●	●	●	●	●	●	●
_____	●	●	●	●	●	●	●
_____	●	●	●	●	●	●	●
_____	●	●	●	●	●	●	●

NOTES

_____

_____

_____

_____

_____

_____

_____

Week 35: Dreams and Goal Setting

"Plans fail for lack of counsel, but with many advisers, they succeed."

Proverbs 15:22 (NIV)

As busy women we sometimes find ourselves in situations where we need to make important decisions. In our homes, businesses, and places of work, we must make informed decisions if we want to succeed in what we do. Proverbs 15:22 suggests the wisdom of seeking advice from others. As Christian women, we are called to seek the counsel of godly and wise people. Emphasis on godly! Instead of relying solely on our own understanding, let us embrace the collective wisdom of those around us. Taking a moment to seek counsel can be the key to successful plans. This may involve learning a thing or two from those who are already successful in the career path we are taking or seeking relationship advice from a couple who have overcome trials together. Let us be open to the perspectives of others and understand that shared wisdom often lights the path to success.

Prayer

Heavenly Father, we thank you for the people around us who inspire us to soar higher. Thank you, dear Lord, for the mentors in our lives who provide advice and counseling. Help us to recognize the importance of seeking counsel in our decision-making and when going through challenges. Help us to be open to the godly advice of those around us and understand that collaboration leads to success. May our plans be positively shaped by the insights of spiritual advisers, friends, family and all who provide counsel. We pray, dear Lord, that you surround us with individuals whose wisdom will help us achieve our goals and ambitions. In the name of Jesus, we pray. Amen.

Related Scriptures for the Week

Proverbs 11:14 (NIV)

"For lack of guidance, a nation falls, but victory is won through many advisers."

Proverbs 12:15 (NIV)

"The way of fools seems right to them, but the wise listen to advice."

Proverbs 24:6 (NIV)

"Surely you need guidance to wage war, and victory is won through many advisers."

Proverbs 20:18 (NIV)

"Plans are established by seeking advice; so if you wage war, obtain guidance."

Proverbs 19:20 (NIV)

"Listen to advice and accept discipline, and at the end you will be counted among the wise."

Proverbs 16:22 (NIV)

"Prudence is a fountain of life to the prudent, but folly brings punishment to fools."

Proverbs 15:31 (NIV)

"Whoever heeds life-giving correction will be at home among the wise."

Proverbs 13:10 (NIV)

"Where there is strife, there is pride, but wisdom is found in those who take advice."

Prayer Tracker

WEEK OF: / /

PRAYER REQUEST	S	M	T	W	T	F	S
_____	○	○	○	○	○	○	○
_____	○	○	○	○	○	○	○
_____	○	○	○	○	○	○	○
_____	○	○	○	○	○	○	○
_____	○	○	○	○	○	○	○
_____	○	○	○	○	○	○	○
_____	○	○	○	○	○	○	○
_____	○	○	○	○	○	○	○
_____	○	○	○	○	○	○	○
_____	○	○	○	○	○	○	○
_____	○	○	○	○	○	○	○
_____	○	○	○	○	○	○	○
_____	○	○	○	○	○	○	○

NOTES

_____

_____

_____

_____

_____

_____

_____

Week 36: Dreams and Goal Setting

"Whatever you do, work at it with all your heart, as working for the Lord, not for human masters, since you know that you will receive an inheritance from the Lord as a reward. It is the Lord Christ you are serving."

Colossians 3:23-24 (NIV)

Colossians 3:23-24 encourages a shift in perspective as we set our goals and as we strive to fulfill them. As women of God, we are called to devote our dreams to God while also giving a wholehearted effort. When we approach our dreams with the perspective that we are doing it for the Lord, a shift occurs. It is like finding purpose in our daily work. Whether in our jobs, volunteer roles, or relationships, working with our whole hearts as if it is an offering to the Lord brings meaning and fulfillment. This perspective reshapes our goals and turns them into opportunities for spiritual growth and a deeper connection with the Lord. As we navigate the demands of life, let us strive to make sure our actions are also matched with dedication and love, knowing that our ultimate reward comes from serving God.

Prayer

Dear God, help us to internalize the wisdom of Colossians 3:23-24 as we set our goals and dreams. We ask that you instill in us a spirit of devotion as we undertake the pursuit of our dreams and aspirations. Lord, may all our endeavors be an offering to you. We pray that you grant us the strength to approach our goals not merely as personal achievements but as acts of worship. In our pursuit of dreams, may our hearts be aligned with your will, O God. Please guide us to work with whole hearts and understand that our efforts are a service to you. We ask, dear Lord, that you grant us the strength to approach each task with dedication in the knowledge that our ultimate reward comes from serving you. In the name of Jesus, we pray. Amen.

Related Scriptures for the Week

Ephesians 6:7-8 (NIV)

"Serve wholeheartedly, as if you were serving the Lord, not people, because you know that the Lord will reward each one for whatever good they do, whether they are slave or free."

1 Corinthians 10:31 (NIV)

"So whether you eat or drink or whatever you do, do it all for the glory of God."

Matthew 6:1-4 (NIV)

"Be careful not to practice your righteousness in front of others to be seen by them. If you do, you will have no reward from your Father in heaven."

2 Timothy 2:15 (NIV)

"Do your best to present yourself to God as one approved, a worker who does not need to be ashamed and who correctly handles the word of truth."

1 Peter 4:10-11 (NIV)

"Each of you should use whatever gift you have received to serve others, as faithful stewards of God's grace in its various forms. If anyone speaks, they should do so as one who speaks the very words of God. If anyone serves, they should do so with the strength God provides, so that in all things God may be praised through Jesus Christ."

Matthew 25:21 (NIV)

"His master replied, 'Well done, good and faithful servant! You have been faithful with a few things; I will put you in charge of many things. Come and share your master's happiness!'"

Hebrews 6:10 (NIV)

"God is not unjust; he will not forget your work and the love you have shown him as you have helped his people and continue to help them."

Revelation 22:12 (NIV)

"Look, I am coming soon! My reward is with me, and I will give to each person according to what they have done."

Prayer Tracker

WEEK OF: / /

PRAYER REQUEST	S	M	T	W	T	F	S
_____	○	○	○	○	○	○	○
_____	○	○	○	○	○	○	○
_____	○	○	○	○	○	○	○
_____	○	○	○	○	○	○	○
_____	○	○	○	○	○	○	○
_____	○	○	○	○	○	○	○
_____	○	○	○	○	○	○	○
_____	○	○	○	○	○	○	○
_____	○	○	○	○	○	○	○
_____	○	○	○	○	○	○	○
_____	○	○	○	○	○	○	○
_____	○	○	○	○	○	○	○
_____	○	○	○	○	○	○	○

NOTES

_____

_____

_____

_____

_____

_____

_____

Week 37: Dreams and Goal Setting

"Commit to the Lord whatever you do, and He will establish your plans."

Proverbs 16:3 (NIV)

As women of purpose, we often find ourselves making plans and setting goals. Proverbs 16:3 provides us with a guiding principle which urges us to include God in our plans. It instructs us to shift our perspective from self-reliance and understanding to working in communion with God. Committing our plans to the Lord is like having a trustworthy guide on our journey. When we do so, we acknowledge His sovereignty over our lives, and as a result, He establishes them according to His perfect will. By inviting Him into our endeavors, we open the door for His guidance and blessings. Let us seek His guidance, surrender our desires, and trust that the path He establishes is far more fulfilling than any plan we could devise without Him.

Prayer

Heavenly Father, as we set our goals and aspirations, help us to remember the wisdom in Proverbs 16:3. We ask you to guide us in committing our plans to you as we seek your guidance and blessings. We acknowledge you as the master planner of our goals and dreams, and we recognize your sovereignty over every aspect of our lives. May our actions align with your purpose, and in our commitment to You, may our paths be established by your wisdom and grace. In the name of Jesus, we pray. Amen.

Related Scriptures for the Week

Psalm 37:5 (NIV)

"Commit your way to the Lord; trust in him, and he will do this.

Proverbs 3:5-6 (NIV)

"Trust in the Lord with all your heart and lean not on your own understanding; in all your ways submit to him, and he will make your paths straight."

Psalm 90:17 (NIV)

"May the favor of the Lord our God rest on us; establish the work of our hands for us—yes, establish the work of our hands."

James 4:13-15 (NIV)

"Now listen, you who say, 'Today or tomorrow we will go to this or that city, spend a year there, carry on business and make money.' Why, you do not even know what will happen tomorrow. What is your life? You are a mist that appears for a little while and then vanishes. Instead, you ought to say, 'If it is the Lord's will, we will live and do this or that.'"

Jeremiah 29:11 (NIV)

"For I know the plans I have for you, declares the Lord, plans for welfare and not for evil, to give you a future and a hope."

1 Corinthians 10:31 (NIV)

"So whether you eat or drink or whatever you do, do it all for the glory of God."

Prayer Tracker

WEEK OF: / /

PRAYER REQUEST	S	M	T	W	T	F	S
_____	○	○	○	○	○	○	○
_____	○	○	○	○	○	○	○
_____	○	○	○	○	○	○	○
_____	○	○	○	○	○	○	○
_____	○	○	○	○	○	○	○
_____	○	○	○	○	○	○	○
_____	○	○	○	○	○	○	○
_____	○	○	○	○	○	○	○
_____	○	○	○	○	○	○	○
_____	○	○	○	○	○	○	○
_____	○	○	○	○	○	○	○
_____	○	○	○	○	○	○	○
_____	○	○	○	○	○	○	○

NOTES

_____
_____
_____
_____
_____
_____
_____

Week 38: Dreams and Goal Setting

"In their hearts, humans plan their course, but the Lord establishes their steps."

Proverbs 16:9 (NIV)

Proverbs 16:9 reveals to us that our dreams and goals, even though they are well-planned, can only find their true direction in God. It reminds us to involve God in every plan and in all our aspirations. We must always seek divine intervention before we start anything or before we pursue our goals. This way, God will grant us the grace and strength needed to navigate the path ahead. As we encounter the complexities of our busy lives, let us recognize the guidance of God in shaping our steps. May we all learn to entrust our plans, dreams, and goals to the Lord. Just as He guided the women in the Bible into fulfilling their purpose, He will establish our course. God, in His love and kindness, will lead us and teach us the way we should go.

Prayer

Dear God, as we make plans and set our course, we invite you into our hearts to help us trust in your guiding hand. We acknowledge that sometimes we want to do things our way, and we repent of this. In the hecticness of our lives, we long to find comfort in the assurance that you establish our steps. Please, Lord, guide us along the path you have set for us, and may our hearts be open to your direction. Just like Moses always turned to you for guidance before he did anything, we pray that we too will always seek your face and involve you before we pursue our goals. We thank you for the promise that when we commit our plans to you, you will establish them. In the name of Jesus, we pray. Amen.

Related Scriptures for the Week

Psalm 37:23 (NIV)

"The Lord makes firm the steps of the one who delights in him."

Jeremiah 10:23 (NIV)

"I know, Lord, that people's lives are not their own; it is not for them to direct their steps."

Proverbs 20:24 (NIV)

"A person's steps are directed by the Lord. How then can anyone understand their own way?"

Proverbs 19:21 (NIV)

"Many are the plans in a person's heart, but it is the Lord's purpose that prevails."

Proverbs 21:1 (NIV)

"In the Lord's hand, the king's heart is a stream of water that he channels toward all who please him."

Psalm 119:105 (NIV)

"Your word is a lamp for my feet, a light on my path."

Prayer Tracker

WEEK OF: / /

PRAYER REQUEST   S   M   T   W   T   F   S

_____

_____

_____

_____

_____

_____

_____

_____

_____

_____

_____

_____

_____

NOTES

_____

_____

_____

_____

_____

_____

_____

Week 39: Dreams and Goal Setting

"I can do all this through Him who gives me strength."

Philippians 4:13 (NIV)

Life's demands often push us to our limits, leaving us feeling overwhelmed and defeated. However, Philippians 4:13 offers encouragement of strength and hope that can help us in our weariness. It is a reassuring promise that, with Christ, we have the power to face any challenge and triumph that comes our way. In the midst of our busy lives, may we be encouraged by this promise to overcome the fear of the unknown, the feeling that we are inferior, and the relentless doubts that sometimes lingers in our minds. Whether it's facing work deadlines, managing family responsibilities, or navigating financial difficulties, may we draw strength from the One who empowers us. May we find confidence in knowing that, through Christ, we are capable of more than we can imagine. In Him, we find strength, grace, and wisdom.

Prayer

Heavenly Father, we thank you for your promise of strength and the grace to accomplish everything that comes our way. As we navigate the challenges of our busy lives, we pray that we may find strength in the promise of Philippians 4:13. Please, Lord, help us to lean on you in times of difficulty and trust that through Christ, we can overcome any obstacle. In our weakness, be our strength, and may your grace be sufficient in every aspect of our lives. Help us, Lord, to face each day with the assurance that you empower us to do all things. In the name of Jesus, we pray. Amen.

Related Scriptures for the Week
Isaiah 40:31 (NIV)

"But those who hope in the Lord will renew their strength. They will soar on wings like eagles; they will run and not grow weary, they will walk and not be faint."

2 Corinthians 12:9 (NIV)

"But he said to me, 'My grace is sufficient for you, for my power is made perfect in weakness.' Therefore I will boast all the more gladly about my weaknesses, so that Christ's power may rest on me."

Psalm 18:32 (NIV)

"It is God who arms me with strength and keeps my way secure."

Ephesians 6:10 (NIV)

"Finally, be strong in the Lord and in his mighty power."

Isaiah 41:10 (NIV)

"So do not fear, for I am with you; do not be dismayed, for I am your God. I will strengthen you and help you; I will uphold you with my righteous right hand."

Psalm 28:7-8 (NIV)

"The Lord is my strength and my shield; my heart trusts in him, and he helps me. My heart leaps for joy, and with my song I praise him."

Colossians 1:11 (NIV)

"Being strengthened with all power according to his glorious might so that you may have great endurance and patience."

Psalm 46:1 (NIV)

"God is our refuge and strength, an ever-present help in trouble."

Prayer Tracker

WEEK OF: / /

PRAYER REQUEST   S   M   T   W   T   F   S

_____

_____

_____

_____

_____

_____

_____

_____

_____

_____

_____

_____

_____

NOTES

_____

_____

_____

_____

_____

_____

_____

Week 40: Gratitude and Joy

"A happy heart makes the face cheerful, but heartache crushes the spirit."

Proverbs 15:13 (NIV)

Proverbs 15:13 shares a simple yet powerful truth. It illustrates how joy has a remarkable effect on our daily lives. While challenges may cast shadows, maintaining a joyful heart can brighten even the gloomiest days. Even when we are overwhelmed, let us remember the impact our attitude can have on those around us. Choosing joy, even in small moments, creates a ripple effect, lifting spirits and spreading light to ourselves and those around us. While it is not easy to maintain a joyful heart in all situations, there are many things we can do to brighten our mood. This may include thinking about the good moments, the love of God, and the little things we have achieved. Think about the positive things all the time and your heart will find joy.

Prayer

Dear God, we thank you for all the good things you have done in our lives and for what you continue to do. As we come before you today, we humbly ask you to teach us the importance of a joyful attitude. Help us, dear Lord, to find moments of happiness even in the midst of busyness. May our attitudes reflect the joy that comes from you. Help us to brighten our faces and the faces of those we encounter. In moments of heartache, let your comfort be our source of enduring joy. In the name of Jesus, we pray. Amen.

Related Scriptures for the Week

Proverbs 17:22 (NIV)

"A cheerful heart is good medicine, but a crushed spirit dries up the bones."

Psalm 30:5 (NIV)

"For his anger lasts only a moment, but his favor lasts a lifetime; weeping may stay for the night, but rejoicing comes in the morning."

Proverbs 12:25 (NIV)

"Anxiety weighs down the heart, but a kind word cheers it up."

Psalm 34:17-18 (NIV)

"The righteous cry out, and the Lord hears them; he delivers them from all their troubles. The Lord is close to the brokenhearted and saves those who are crushed in spirit."

Proverbs 16:24 (NIV)

"Gracious words are a honeycomb, sweet to the soul and healing to the bones."

Isaiah 41:10 (NIV)

"So do not fear, for I am with you; do not be dismayed, for I am your God. I will strengthen you and help you; I will uphold you with my righteous right hand."

Psalm 42:11 (NIV)

"Why, my soul, are you downcast? Why so disturbed within me? Put your hope in God, for I will yet praise him, my Savior and my God."

Prayer Tracker

WEEK OF: / /

PRAYER REQUEST	S	M	T	W	T	F	S
_____	○	○	○	○	○	○	○
_____	○	○	○	○	○	○	○
_____	○	○	○	○	○	○	○
_____	○	○	○	○	○	○	○
_____	○	○	○	○	○	○	○
_____	○	○	○	○	○	○	○
_____	○	○	○	○	○	○	○
_____	○	○	○	○	○	○	○
_____	○	○	○	○	○	○	○
_____	○	○	○	○	○	○	○
_____	○	○	○	○	○	○	○
_____	○	○	○	○	○	○	○
_____	○	○	○	○	○	○	○

NOTES

_____
_____
_____
_____
_____
_____
_____

Week 41: Gratitude and Joy

"Is anyone among you in trouble? Let them pray. Is anyone happy? Let them sing songs of praise."

James 5:13 (NIV)

Life unfolds with a mix of experiences. Sometimes we experience moments of joy, and other times we encounter times of trouble. But amid all these, James 5:13 reveals to us that we need to find the connection between prayer, praise, and joy. When we are going through tough times, we are called to pray. In the busy chapters of our lives, prayer becomes a constant. Through prayer, we connect with God and we are able to thank Him for being with us in every situation. Whether in moments of victory or challenges, this verse encourages us to turn to God so that we may find joy in our hearts. So, in the midst of our busy schedules, let us cultivate a habit of turning to prayer in times of trouble and expressing gratitude in moments of joy.

Prayer

Heavenly Father, we praise you for your faithfulness, mercy, and love which endure forever. May our praises and gratitude to you not be limited by the circumstances we are going through but inspired by your unchanging character. Lord, we pray that you teach us to turn to you with praise and thanksgiving, whether in moments of trouble or joy. Help us cultivate a heart of gratitude and a spirit of dependence on you. In the hustle of our days, let prayer be our guide to your joy and gratitude. In the name of Jesus, we pray. Amen.

Related Scriptures for the Week

Philippians 4:6 (NIV)

"Do not be anxious about anything, but in every situation, by prayer and petition, with thanksgiving, present your requests to God."

Psalm 100:2 (NIV)

"Worship the Lord with gladness; come before him with joyful songs."

Psalm 50:14-15 (NIV)

"Sacrifice thank offerings to God, fulfill your vows to the Most High, and call on me in the day of trouble; I will deliver you, and you will honor me."

1 Chronicles 16:23-24 (NIV)

"Sing to the Lord, all the earth; proclaim his salvation day after day. Declare his glory among the nations, his marvelous deeds among all peoples."

Ephesians 5:19 (NIV)

"Speak to one another with psalms, hymns, and songs from the Spirit. Sing and make music from your heart to the Lord."

Matthew 6:6 (NIV)

"But when you pray, go into your room, close the door and pray to your Father, who is unseen. Then your Father, who sees what is done in secret, will reward you."

Psalm 118:24 (NIV)

"This is the day the Lord has made; let us rejoice and be glad in it."

Prayer Tracker

WEEK OF: / /

PRAYER REQUEST	S	M	T	W	T	F	S
_____	○	○	○	○	○	○	○
_____	○	○	○	○	○	○	○
_____	○	○	○	○	○	○	○
_____	○	○	○	○	○	○	○
_____	○	○	○	○	○	○	○
_____	○	○	○	○	○	○	○
_____	○	○	○	○	○	○	○
_____	○	○	○	○	○	○	○
_____	○	○	○	○	○	○	○
_____	○	○	○	○	○	○	○
_____	○	○	○	○	○	○	○
_____	○	○	○	○	○	○	○
_____	○	○	○	○	○	○	○

NOTES

_____

_____

_____

_____

_____

_____

_____

Week 42: Gratitude and Joy

"When times are good, be happy; but when times are bad, consider this: God has made the one as well as the other. Therefore, no one can discover anything about their future."

Ecclesiastes 7:14 (NIV)

God created different seasons, and all of them are with their own purpose. The fact that we are Christian women does not mean that we won't face challenges in life. In fact, we are the most targeted by the enemy. But take heart. In the midst of our busy lives, this verse encourages us to embrace both the highs and lows. It reminds us that every season serves a purpose and we need to embrace them with joy and gratitude. Romans 8:28 tells us that God works everything for our good. Therefore, we must thank Him even when situations are hard so that He can bring out the goodness behind every season. And as we navigate through bad and good times, let us remember that we are not alone. In moments of joy, let us savor the goodness, and in times of difficulty, let us find comfort in the understanding that God is at work to shape our stories in unique and meaningful ways.

Prayer

Dear God, we thank you for the gifts of seasons and time. We know that you created every season for a divine purpose and for our good, though sometimes we are blind to the good behind the situations we go through. As we reflect on Ecclesiastes 7:14, please grant us the wisdom to appreciate the diversity of our experiences. In moments of joy, may we celebrate your goodness, and in times of challenge, may we find comfort in your presence. Teach us, O Lord, to give thanks in every season of our lives and to find joy in them. Help us to trust your plan, for we recognize that every season is part of our lives. In our busy days, may we navigate both the good and the bad with gratitude and faith. In the name of Jesus, we pray. Amen.

Related Scriptures for the Week

Proverbs 3:5-6 (NIV)

"Trust in the Lord with all your heart and lean not on your own understanding; in all your ways submit to him, and he will make your paths straight."

James 1:2-3 (NIV)

"Consider it pure joy, my brothers and sisters, whenever you face trials of many kinds because you know that the testing of your faith produces perseverance."

Romans 8:28 (NIV)

"And we know that in all things God works for the good of those who love him, who have been called according to his purpose."

2 Corinthians 4:17 (NIV)

"For our light and momentary troubles are achieving for us an eternal glory that far outweighs them all."

Job 2:10 (NIV)

"Shall we accept good from God, and not trouble? In all this, Job did not sin in what he said."

Isaiah 45:7 (NIV)

"I form the light and create darkness, I bring prosperity and create disaster; I, the Lord, do all these things."

Lamentations 3:22-23 (NIV)

"Because of the Lord's great love we are not consumed, for his compassions never fail. They are new every morning; great is your faithfulness."

Prayer Tracker

WEEK OF: / /

PRAYER REQUEST	S	M	T	W	T	F	S
_____	○	○	○	○	○	○	○
_____	○	○	○	○	○	○	○
_____	○	○	○	○	○	○	○
_____	○	○	○	○	○	○	○
_____	○	○	○	○	○	○	○
_____	○	○	○	○	○	○	○
_____	○	○	○	○	○	○	○
_____	○	○	○	○	○	○	○
_____	○	○	○	○	○	○	○
_____	○	○	○	○	○	○	○
_____	○	○	○	○	○	○	○
_____	○	○	○	○	○	○	○
_____	○	○	○	○	○	○	○

NOTES

_____

_____

_____

_____

_____

_____

_____

Week 43: Gratitude and Joy

"Give thanks in all circumstances; for this is God's will for you in Christ Jesus."

1 Thessalonians 5:18 (NIV)

Amid our busy schedules and hectic lives, we are called to give thanks because it is the will of God for all of us. 1 Thessalonians 5:18 reminds us that gratitude is not circumstantial; it is an emotion that is embedded in our faith in God. It is an intentional act of being grateful regardless of our circumstances because we know that God will help us out. It is like a key that unlocks joy, even during challenging times. This verse challenges us to cultivate a thankful heart, not just when things are easy but in every circumstance. In our hectic lives, let us pause to appreciate the blessings, both big and small, trusting that a heart steeped in gratitude aligns with God's will for us.

Prayer

Heavenly Father, we come before you today asking that you guide us in cultivating a spirit of gratitude. Teach us, Lord, to give thanks in all circumstances and to trust your plan for our lives. In moments of ease and difficulty, may gratitude be our response. In the midst of our hectic lives, let our thankful hearts testify of your goodness, faithfulness, and love. Please, Lord, we pray that you help us to give thanks always as a reflection of your will in our lives. In the name of Jesus, we pray. Amen.

Related Scriptures for the Week

Ephesians 5:20 (NIV)

"always giving thanks to God the Father for everything, in the name of our Lord Jesus Christ."

Colossians 3:17 (NIV)

"And whatever you do, whether in word or deed, do it all in the name of the Lord Jesus, giving thanks to God the Father through him."

Psalm 106:1 (NIV)

"Praise the Lord. Give thanks to the Lord, for he is good; his love endures forever."

Psalm 136:26 (NIV)

"Give thanks to the God of heaven. His love endures forever."

1 Chronicles 16:34 (NIV)

"Give thanks to the Lord, for he is good; his love endures forever."

Psalm 95:2 (NIV)

"Let us come before him with thanksgiving and extol him with music and song."

Colossians 4:2 (NIV)

"Devote yourselves to prayer, being watchful and thankful."

Prayer Tracker

WEEK OF: / /

PRAYER REQUEST	S	M	T	W	T	F	S
_____	○	○	○	○	○	○	○
_____	○	○	○	○	○	○	○
_____	○	○	○	○	○	○	○
_____	○	○	○	○	○	○	○
_____	○	○	○	○	○	○	○
_____	○	○	○	○	○	○	○
_____	○	○	○	○	○	○	○
_____	○	○	○	○	○	○	○
_____	○	○	○	○	○	○	○
_____	○	○	○	○	○	○	○
_____	○	○	○	○	○	○	○
_____	○	○	○	○	○	○	○
_____	○	○	○	○	○	○	○

NOTES

_____

_____

_____

_____

_____

_____

_____

Week 44: Courage and Resilience

"Be strong and courageous. Do not be afraid or terrified because of them, for the Lord your God goes with you; He will never leave you nor forsake you."

Deuteronomy 31:6 (NIV)

Life can be a tricky journey with challenges that require courage and resilience. Life's hard moments may leave us feeling afraid and terrified. However, Deuteronomy 31:6 encourages us that even though hardship and challenges come our way, we are not alone. God is always with us, and we can find courage and strength in His presence. He holds our hands through the ups and downs of life and walks with us through them all. As we navigate the busy and demanding days, let us draw strength from the assurance that God is with us and will never forsake us no matter what happens. In His presence, we find the courage to face uncertainties.

Prayer

Dear God, as we bow our heads before you in adoration and reverence, we thank you for your assurance in Deuteronomy 31:6 that you will never leave us nor forsake us. This assurance gives us hope and courage to face life's trials with resilience. Please, Lord, instill in us the courage and resilience needed for life's journey. Help us to be strong and fearless in the knowledge that your presence goes with us. In moments of challenge, may your support be our source of strength. As we face the demands of our busy lives, let courage be our companion, and may we find resilience in your constant presence. In the name of Jesus, we pray. Amen.

Related Scriptures for the Week

Joshua 1:9 (NIV)

"Have I not commanded you? Be strong and courageous. Do not be afraid; do not be discouraged, for the Lord your God will be with you wherever you go."

Isaiah 41:10 (NIV)

"So do not fear, for I am with you; do not be dismayed, for I am your God. I will strengthen you and help you; I will uphold you with my righteous right hand."

Psalm 23:4 (NIV)

"Even though I walk through the darkest valley, I will fear no evil, for you are with me; your rod and your staff, they comfort me."

Hebrews 13:5 (NIV)

"Keep your lives free from the love of money and be content with what you have, because God has said, 'Never will I leave you; never will I forsake you.'"

1 Chronicles 28:20 (NIV)

"David also said to Solomon his son, 'Be strong and courageous, and do the work. Do not be afraid or discouraged, for the Lord God, my God, is with you. He will not fail you or forsake you until all the work for the service of the temple of the Lord is finished.'"

Prayer Tracker

WEEK OF: / /

PRAYER REQUEST	S	M	T	W	T	F	S
_____	●	●	●	●	●	●	●
_____	●	●	●	●	●	●	●
_____	●	●	●	●	●	●	●
_____	●	●	●	●	●	●	●
_____	●	●	●	●	●	●	●
_____	●	●	●	●	●	●	●
_____	●	●	●	●	●	●	●
_____	●	●	●	●	●	●	●
_____	●	●	●	●	●	●	●
_____	●	●	●	●	●	●	●
_____	●	●	●	●	●	●	●
_____	●	●	●	●	●	●	●
_____	●	●	●	●	●	●	●

NOTES

_____

_____

_____

_____

_____

_____

_____

Week 45: Courage and Resilience

"Therefore, my dear brothers and sisters, stand firm. Let nothing move you. Always give yourselves fully to the work of the Lord, because you know that your labor in the Lord is not in vain."

1 Corinthians 15:58 (NIV)

1 Corinthians 15:58 extends an enduring call to courage and resilience in the face of trials and tribulation. Life's demands often require perseverance and steadfastness. As women of God, we are encouraged not to be shaken by difficulties but to persist in the work of the Lord. And the promise embedded in this scripture is powerful. We are told that our efforts, our struggles, and our resilience in God's work are not in vain. This is a call to stand firm and to be unwavering in our commitment to God's work amid the challenges that surround our lives. Our resilience and courage in fulfilling God's purpose are

not fruitless. Even though it may take long, God will ultimately reward us. As we journey through our busy lives, may we find strength and purpose in dedicating ourselves fully to the work of the Lord.

Prayer

Heavenly Father, we thank you for your steadfast and timeless encouragement in 1 Corinthians 15:18. Lord, we humbly ask you to grant us the courage to stand firm, unshaken by life's challenges. In moments of difficulty, help us to give ourselves wholeheartedly to your work. We pray, dear Lord, that you guide us in standing firm and giving ourselves fully to your work. In the busyness of life, may we find perseverance in the knowledge that our labor in you is not in vain. Please, Lord, we ask that you grant us the strength to remain steadfast and may our efforts bring glory to your name. In every task, may we find purpose and fulfillment in serving you. In the name of Jesus, we pray. Amen.

Related Scriptures for the Week

Galatians 6:9 (NIV)

"Let us not become weary in doing good, for at the proper time we will reap a harvest if we do not give up."

1 Corinthians 16:13 (NIV)

"Be on your guard; stand firm in the faith; be courageous; be strong."

Colossians 3:23-24 (NIV)

"Whatever you do, work at it with all your heart, as working for the Lord, not for human masters, since you know that you will receive an inheritance from the Lord as a reward. It is the Lord Christ you are serving."

2 Timothy 4:7-8 (NIV)

"I have fought the good fight, I have finished the race, I have kept the faith. Now there is in store for me the crown of righteousness, which the Lord, the righteous Judge, will award to me on that day—and not only to me, but also to all who have longed for his appearing."

Hebrews 10:36 (NIV)

"You need to persevere so that when you have done the will of God, you will receive what he has promised."

1 Thessalonians 3:13 (NIV)

"May he strengthen your hearts so that you will be blameless and holy in the presence of our God and Father when our Lord Jesus comes with all his holy ones."

2 Thessalonians 2:15 (NIV)

"So then, brothers and sisters, stand firm and hold fast to the teachings we passed on to you, whether by word of mouth or by letter."

Revelation 2:10 (NIV)

"Do not be afraid of what you are about to suffer. I tell you, the devil will put some of you in prison to test you, and you will suffer persecution for ten days. Be faithful, even to the point of death, and I will give you life as your victor's crown."

Prayer Tracker

WEEK OF: / /

PRAYER REQUEST	S	M	T	W	T	F	S
_____	○	○	○	○	○	○	○
_____	○	○	○	○	○	○	○
_____	○	○	○	○	○	○	○
_____	○	○	○	○	○	○	○
_____	○	○	○	○	○	○	○
_____	○	○	○	○	○	○	○
_____	○	○	○	○	○	○	○
_____	○	○	○	○	○	○	○
_____	○	○	○	○	○	○	○
_____	○	○	○	○	○	○	○
_____	○	○	○	○	○	○	○
_____	○	○	○	○	○	○	○
_____	○	○	○	○	○	○	○

NOTES

_____

_____

_____

_____

_____

_____

_____

Week 46: Courage and Resilience

"When I am afraid, I put my trust in you. In God, whose word I praise—in God I trust and am not afraid. What can mere mortals do to me?"

Psalms 56:3-4 (NIV)

Life often presents moments that stir fear within us. The fear of the unknown, fear of challenges, fear of the opinions of others, and so much more can scare us silly. However, this wonderful Bible verse is a declaration of trust in the face of fear. It is a reassuring whisper that in God, we find a refuge that extends beyond our anxieties. Our trust in God banishes fear, worry, and anxiety from our hearts. When we trust in God, He renews our strength and grants us the grace to face life with courage and resilience. As we navigate the crazy days, let us always remember to anchor our trust in God and understand that, with Him, we need not be afraid.

Prayer

Dear God, we come before you in prayer for courage and resilience. We find comfort in the words of wisdom found in Psalms 56:3-4. In moments of fear and uncertainty, we seek your refuge Lord. Help us to put our trust in you and to find strength in your promises. In the midst of life's uncertainties, may our trust in you overshadow any fear that tries to take hold. Please, Lord, we ask that you guide us to walk in confidence, knowing that with you, we are secure. In the name of Jesus, we pray. Amen.

Related Scriptures for the Week

Psalm 34:4 (NIV)

"I sought the Lord, and he answered me; he delivered me from all my fears."

Psalm 27:1 (NIV)

"The Lord is my light and my salvation—whom shall I fear? The Lord is the stronghold of my life—of whom shall I be afraid?"

Psalm 118:6 (NIV)

"The Lord is with me; I will not be afraid. What can mere mortals do to me?"

Psalm 55:22 (NIV)

"Cast your cares on the Lord and he will sustain you; he will never let the righteous be shaken."

John 14:27 (NIV)

"Peace I leave with you; my peace I give you. I do not give to you as the world gives. Do not let your hearts be troubled and do not be afraid."

Prayer Tracker

WEEK OF: / /

PRAYER REQUEST	S	M	T	W	T	F	S
_____	◯	◯	◯	◯	◯	◯	◯
_____	◯	◯	◯	◯	◯	◯	◯
_____	◯	◯	◯	◯	◯	◯	◯
_____	◯	◯	◯	◯	◯	◯	◯
_____	◯	◯	◯	◯	◯	◯	◯
_____	◯	◯	◯	◯	◯	◯	◯
_____	◯	◯	◯	◯	◯	◯	◯
_____	◯	◯	◯	◯	◯	◯	◯
_____	◯	◯	◯	◯	◯	◯	◯
_____	◯	◯	◯	◯	◯	◯	◯
_____	◯	◯	◯	◯	◯	◯	◯
_____	◯	◯	◯	◯	◯	◯	◯
_____	◯	◯	◯	◯	◯	◯	◯

NOTES

_____
_____
_____
_____
_____
_____
_____

Week 47: Courage and Resilience

"So do not fear, for I am with you; do not be dismayed, for I am your God. I will strengthen you and help you; I will uphold you with my righteous right hand. "All who rage against you will surely be ashamed and disgraced; those who oppose you will be as nothing and perish.

Though you search for your enemies, you will not find them. Those who wage war against you will be as nothing at all. For I am the Lord your God who takes hold of your right hand and says to you, do not fear; I will help you."

Isaiah 41:10-13 (NIV)

Life is a journey filled with uncertainties and moments that evoke fear within our hearts. But God's Word in Isaiah 41:10-13 reassures us that we can always count on God's help because He is always with us. God, in His boundless love, promises to be with us, to offer us strength, to help us, and to offer a support that upholds us with His righteous hand. The promise to strengthen, help, and uphold us echoes through the challenges we face. When fear knocks at the door, let our response be to remember these words and find courage in the presence of our God. With His help, everything is possible. Despite the storms, let us anchor ourselves in the embrace of the Lord and find strength in His loving arms.

Prayer

Heavenly Father, we thank you for the promise to be with us and uphold us in every situation. In moments of fear and uncertainty, we turn to you, our refuge and strength. You have always been our strength and our ever-present help in times of distress. Father, we humbly ask you to help us remember your assurance every time we encounter a challenge. We pray that you strengthen us, uphold us, and guide us with your righteous right hand. As we navigate the craziness of life, may your presence be a source of courage, and may we find confidence in your unwavering support. In the name of Jesus, we pray. Amen.

Related Scriptures for the Week

Psalm 91:4 (NIV)

"He will cover you with his feathers, and under his wings you will find refuge; his faithfulness will be your shield and rampart."

Psalm 46:1 (NIV)

"God is our refuge and strength, an ever-present help in trouble."

Isaiah 43:2 (NIV)

"When you pass through the waters, I will be with you; and when you pass through the rivers, they will not sweep over you. When you walk through the fire, you will not be burned; the flames will not set you ablaze."

Joshua 1:9 (NIV)

"Have I not commanded you? Be strong and courageous. Do not be afraid; do not be discouraged, for the Lord your God will be with you wherever you go."

Romans 8:31 (NIV)

"What, then, shall we say in response to these things? If God is for us, who can be against us?"

Prayer Tracker

WEEK OF: / /

PRAYER REQUEST	S	M	T	W	T	F	S
_____	●	●	●	●	●	●	●
_____	●	●	●	●	●	●	●
_____	●	●	●	●	●	●	●
_____	●	●	●	●	●	●	●
_____	●	●	●	●	●	●	●
_____	●	●	●	●	●	●	●
_____	●	●	●	●	●	●	●
_____	●	●	●	●	●	●	●
_____	●	●	●	●	●	●	●
_____	●	●	●	●	●	●	●
_____	●	●	●	●	●	●	●
_____	●	●	●	●	●	●	●
_____	●	●	●	●	●	●	●

NOTES

_____
_____
_____
_____
_____
_____
_____
_____

Week 48: Courage and Resilience

"For the Spirit God gave us does not make us timid, but gives us power, love and self-discipline."

2 Timothy 1:7 (NIV)

With so much going on, fear may knock on our doors, but this verse invites us to answer with the power of God's Spirit. As women of God, we are not defined by timidity; we are equipped with divine strength, love, and discipline. In our hectic lives, we are challenged to unleash the attributes of God within us, including courage and resilience. The Word of God in 2 Timothy 1:7 reminds us that fear is not our inheritance from God. We have inherited His strength which surpasses human limitations. Therefore, let us tap into this God-given power to overcome our fears. May we walk boldly, knowing that fear has no dominion over the strength that God has given us.

Prayer

Dear God, we thank for you giving us a spirit not of fear but of courage and resilience. We thank you, dear Lord, for replacing our fears with power, courage, and strength. As we bow before you today, we seek your Spirit to cast out fear and anxiety. In moments of uncertainty, let your strength and power be our refuge. May your Spirit empower us to face life's challenges with courage and confidence, O God. Guide us in using the gifts you have bestowed upon us to overcome fear, knowing that we are more than conquerors through Christ. In the name of Jesus, we pray. Amen.

Related Scriptures for the Week

1 John 4:18 (NIV)

"There is no fear in love. But perfect love drives out fear because fear has to do with punishment. The one who fears is not made perfect in love."

Romans 8:15 (NIV)

"The Spirit you received does not make you slaves, so that you live in fear again; rather, the Spirit you received brought about your adoption to sonship. And by him, we cry, 'Abba, Father.'"

2 Corinthians 10:4 (NIV)

"The weapons we fight with are not the weapons of the world. On the contrary, they have divine power to demolish strongholds."

Romans 8:37 (NIV)

"No, in all these things we are more than conquerors through him who loved us."

Philippians 4:13 (NIV)

"I can do all this through him who gives me strength."

2 Corinthians 3:17 (NIV)

"Now the Lord is the Spirit, and where the Spirit of the Lord is, there is freedom."

Prayer Tracker

WEEK OF: / /

PRAYER REQUEST	S	M	T	W	T	F	S
_____	●	●	●	●	●	●	●
_____	●	●	●	●	●	●	●
_____	●	●	●	●	●	●	●
_____	●	●	●	●	●	●	●
_____	●	●	●	●	●	●	●
_____	●	●	●	●	●	●	●
_____	●	●	●	●	●	●	●
_____	●	●	●	●	●	●	●
_____	●	●	●	●	●	●	●
_____	●	●	●	●	●	●	●
_____	●	●	●	●	●	●	●
_____	●	●	●	●	●	●	●
_____	●	●	●	●	●	●	●

NOTES

_____

_____

_____

_____

_____

_____

_____

_____

Week 49: Serving Others

"Do not withhold good from those to whom it is due,
when it is in your power to act."

Proverbs 3:27 (NIV)

Within our capacity lies the ability to bring goodness into the lives of others. The craziness of life can sometimes distract us from the simple yet profound act of kindness. There are moments when we hold the power to bring a smile to someone's face but we fail to do so because we are too busy chasing our dreams. Proverbs 3:27 urges us not to withhold what is good from those who desperately need it. Serving others through acts of kindness is an expression of the love and compassion we have received from a generous God. It could be a simple act of kindness, a gesture of love, a helping hand, or a word of encouragement. As we navigate our days, let us embrace the opportunities to extend love and kindness.

Prayer

Heavenly Father, we humble ourselves before you today asking that you teach us the beauty of kindness. We ask that you open our eyes to the opportunities to serve others and grant us the willingness to extend kindness and goodness to those around us. In our busy lives, may we not withhold acts of love when it is within our power to act. Fill our hearts with compassion and generosity, and guide us to be sources of positivity in the lives of others. May our actions reflect your love and grace. In the name of Jesus, we pray. Amen.

Related Scriptures for the Week

Matthew 5:42 (NIV):

"Give to the one who asks you, and do not turn away from the one who wants to borrow from you."

Luke 6:38 (NIV):

"Give, and it will be given to you. A good measure, pressed down, shaken together and running over, will be poured into your lap. For with the measure you use, it will be measured to you."

Proverbs 19:17 (NIV):

"Whoever is kind to the poor lends to the Lord, and he will reward them for what they have done."

Hebrews 13:16 (NIV):

"And do not forget to do good and to share with others, for with such sacrifices God is pleased."

James 2:15-16 (NIV):

"Suppose a brother or a sister is without clothes and daily food. If one of you says to them, 'Go in peace; keep warm and well fed,' but does nothing about their physical needs, what good is it?"

Proverbs 14:21 (NIV):

"It is a sin to despise one's neighbor, but blessed is the one who is kind to the needy."

Prayer Tracker

WEEK OF: / /

PRAYER REQUEST	S	M	T	W	T	F	S
_____	○	○	○	○	○	○	○
_____	○	○	○	○	○	○	○
_____	○	○	○	○	○	○	○
_____	○	○	○	○	○	○	○
_____	○	○	○	○	○	○	○
_____	○	○	○	○	○	○	○
_____	○	○	○	○	○	○	○
_____	○	○	○	○	○	○	○
_____	○	○	○	○	○	○	○
_____	○	○	○	○	○	○	○
_____	○	○	○	○	○	○	○
_____	○	○	○	○	○	○	○
_____	○	○	○	○	○	○	○

NOTES

_____

_____

_____

_____

_____

_____

_____

Week 50: Serving Others

"My command is this: Love each other as I have loved you."

John 15:12 (NIV)

In John 15:12, Jesus commands us to extend the love that He has shown us: a sacrificial and unconditional love. When we reflect on the love that Jesus showed us, we find that it was a kind of love marked by selfless service. As women of God, we are called to emulate this love in our interactions with one another. Love, according to Christ's example, is an active force that serves, uplifts, and meets the needs of others. In the midst of our busy lives, we are called to extend the same love we receive from Christ to those around us. This love is not just a feeling but an action that involves serving and caring for others. As we navigate our days, let us embrace the challenge to love sacrificially.

Prayer

Dear Lord, we lift our hearts to you asking that you help us to grasp the depth of your command to love one another. Teach us, O God, to love one another as Christ has loved us, not only in words but in our actions and service to others. In our busy lives, may our actions be a reflection of your sacrificial love. Dear Lord, we ask that you equip us to serve others with compassion and selflessness and create a community of love and service. In the name of Jesus, we pray. Amen.

Related Scriptures for the Week

John 13:34-35 (NIV):

"A new command I give you: Love one another. As I have loved you, so you must love one another. By this everyone will know that you are my disciples if you love one another."

1 John 4:11 (NIV):

"Dear friends, since God so loved us, we also ought to love one another."

Romans 13:8 (NIV):

"Let no debt remain outstanding, except the continuing debt to love one another, for whoever loves others has fulfilled the law."

1 Peter 4:8 (NIV):

"Above all, love each other deeply because love covers over a multitude of sins."

Ephesians 5:2 (NIV):

"And walk in the way of love, just as Christ loved us and gave himself up for us as a fragrant offering and sacrifice to God."

1 John 3:23 (NIV):

"And this is his command: to believe in the name of his Son, Jesus Christ, and to love one another as he commanded us."

Colossians 3:14 (NIV):

"And over all these virtues put on love, which binds them all together in perfect unity."

1 Corinthians 13:13 (NIV):

"And now these three remain: faith, hope, and love. But the greatest of these is love."

Prayer Tracker

WEEK OF:　/　/

PRAYER REQUEST	S	M	T	W	T	F	S
_____	○	○	○	○	○	○	○
_____	○	○	○	○	○	○	○
_____	○	○	○	○	○	○	○
_____	○	○	○	○	○	○	○
_____	○	○	○	○	○	○	○
_____	○	○	○	○	○	○	○
_____	○	○	○	○	○	○	○
_____	○	○	○	○	○	○	○
_____	○	○	○	○	○	○	○
_____	○	○	○	○	○	○	○
_____	○	○	○	○	○	○	○
_____	○	○	○	○	○	○	○
_____	○	○	○	○	○	○	○

NOTES

_____

_____

_____

_____

_____

_____

_____

Week 51: Serving Others

"Share with the Lord's people who are in need. Practice hospitality."

Romans 12:13 (NIV)

Romans 12:13 encourages a spirit of hospitality and service. Hospitality in the biblical context is an attitude of openness, generosity, and our willingness to share whatever we have with those in need. It is a heart devoted to serving others with a welcoming heart. Whether it is extending kindness to a stranger or generously sharing our resources, these actions embody the spirit of hospitality. In our busy lives, we are called to share what we have with those in need, both materially and emotionally. May our hospitality become powerful expressions of service and turn our homes and hearts into welcoming spaces. In practicing hospitality, we not only meet the needs of others but also create a community that reflects the love of Christ.

Prayer

Heavenly Father, we humbly ask you to instill in our hearts a spirit of generosity and openness so that we may serve others with a welcoming heart. Guide us, O Lord, to share with those in need and to practice generosity in our homes and hearts. In the busyness of our lives, help us to be attentive to the needs of others. We give ourselves to you so that you can use us as vessels of kindness and generosity. In our acts of kindness and hospitality, may your name be glorified. In the name of Jesus, we pray. Amen.

Related Scriptures for the Week

Hebrews 13:2 (NIV):

"Do not forget to show hospitality to strangers, for by so doing some people have shown hospitality to angels without knowing it."

1 Peter 4:9 (NIV):

"Offer hospitality to one another without grumbling."

Matthew 25:35 (NIV):

"For I was hungry and you gave me something to eat, I was thirsty and you gave me something to drink, I was a stranger and you invited me in."

Luke 14:13-14 (NIV):

"But when you give a banquet, invite the poor, the crippled, the lame, the blind, and you will be blessed. Although they cannot repay you, you will be repaid at the resurrection of the righteous."

Proverbs 25:21-22 (NIV):

"If your enemy is hungry, give him food to eat; if he is thirsty, give him water to drink. In doing this, you will heap burning coals on his head, and the Lord will reward you."

Matthew 10:42 (NIV):

"And if anyone gives even a cup of cold water to one of these little ones who is my disciple, truly I tell you, that person will certainly not lose their reward."

Prayer Tracker

WEEK OF: / /

PRAYER REQUEST   S   M   T   W   T   F   S

_____

_____

_____

_____

_____

_____

_____

_____

_____

_____

_____

_____

_____

NOTES

_____

_____

_____

_____

_____

_____

_____

Week 52: Serving Others

"Therefore, as we have opportunity, let us do good to all people, especially to those who belong to the family of believers."

Galatians 6:10 (NIV)

Life often presents us with countless chances to make a positive impact, and Galatians 6:10 encourages us to embrace them. Service, according to God's Word, is not limited by circumstances. Rather, it is a call to extend kindness, love, and assistance to everyone we encounter. The call to do good is not a burden but an invitation to participate in the joy and fulfillment that comes from serving others. Let us be intentional in seeking opportunities to do good. Serving others is a communal responsibility among believers. It encourages mutual support and care within the community of faith. There are many women hurting out there. God has chosen us to extend kindness and love to them.

Prayer

Dear God, as we strive to be like Christ, we are inspired by the wisdom of Galatians 6:10 which urges us to do good to all people, especially to those within the family of believers. Father, we ask you to open our eyes to the opportunities you provide for us to serve and extend kindness. May we seize every opportunity to extend love and support. In the midst of our busy lives, may our actions be a reflection of your love and grace. Thank you, dear Lord, for the privilege of serving others. In the name of Jesus, we pray. Amen.

Related Scriptures for the Week

Matthew 5:16 (NIV):

"In the same way, let your light shine before others, that they may see your good deeds and glorify your Father in heaven."

James 1:27 (NIV):

"Religion that God our Father accepts as pure and faultless is this: to look after orphans and widows in their distress and to keep oneself from being polluted by the world."

1 John 3:17-18 (NIV):

"If anyone has material possessions and sees a brother or sister in need but has no pity on them, how can the love of God be in that person? Dear children, let us not love with words or speech but with actions and in truth."

Matthew 25:40 (NIV):

"The King will reply, 'Truly I tell you, whatever you did for one of the least of these brothers and sisters of mine, you did for me.'"

1 Timothy 6:18 (NIV):

"Command them to do good, to be rich in good deeds, and to be generous and willing to share."

2 Corinthians 9:7 (NIV):

"Each of you should give what you have decided in your heart to give, not reluctantly or under compulsion, for God loves a cheerful giver."

Prayer Tracker

WEEK OF: / /

PRAYER REQUEST	S	M	T	W	T	F	S
_____	●	●	●	●	●	●	●
_____	●	●	●	●	●	●	●
_____	●	●	●	●	●	●	●
_____	●	●	●	●	●	●	●
_____	●	●	●	●	●	●	●
_____	●	●	●	●	●	●	●
_____	●	●	●	●	●	●	●
_____	●	●	●	●	●	●	●
_____	●	●	●	●	●	●	●
_____	●	●	●	●	●	●	●
_____	●	●	●	●	●	●	●
_____	●	●	●	●	●	●	●
_____	●	●	●	●	●	●	●

NOTES

_____

_____

_____

_____

_____

_____

_____

—